D1231721

Pen-Portraits of the Prophets

By
BERNARD C. CLAUSEN, D.D.
Pastor, First Baptist Church, Syracuse, N. Y.
Author of "Pen-Portraits of the Twelve," "Preach It Again," "The Miracle of Me," etc.

New York   Chicago
Fleming H. Revell Company
London and Edinburgh

Printed in the United States of America

New York: 158 Fifth Avenue
Chicago: 17 North Wabash Ave.
London: 21 Paternoster Square
Edinburgh: 75 Princes Street

PEN-PORTRAITS OF THE PROPHETS

BERNARD C. CLAUSEN, D. D.

Pen-Portraits of the Prophets $1.50

The Technique of the Minister $1.25

Pen-Portraits of the Twelve $1.50

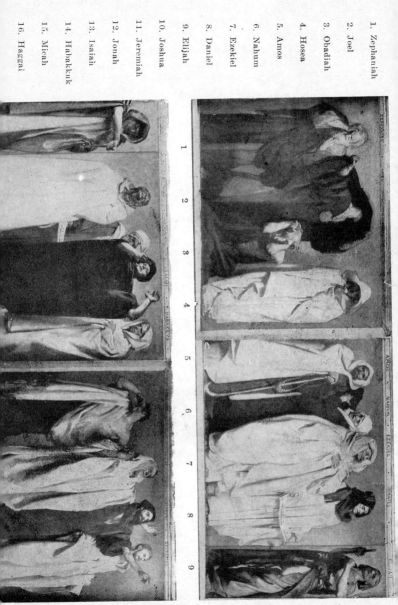

1. Zephaniah
2. Joel
3. Obadiah
4. Hosea
5. Amos
6. Nahum
7. Ezekiel
8. Daniel
9. Elijah
10. Joshua
11. Jeremiah
12. Jonah
13. Isaiah
14. Habakkuk
15. Micah
16. Haggai

To the Man
Who Was My Prophet
FRANK ORSON BELDEN

FOREWORD

HERE are prophets!

But on these pages they appear not as documents which form parts of a sacred book. Nor as representatives of great epochs in a nation's life. Nor as theological achievements in mankind's search for God.

Here they are human preachers, struggling to say their words of truth and inspiration to the people who surround them. These are pen-portraits. The backgrounds are incidental. The faces and the forms are the important things.

So we must begin by putting aside all those involved critical questions of documentary sources and historical records. Literary comparisons and analyses are not vital here. Even that vast pageant of power which the nations were acting out while these men were at work, must be made subordinate to their own personal dramas.

If this process of cutting away the critical and historical and literary considerations requires any justification, it may be fairly said that such questions have been fully discussed in a hundred books. Perhaps there is place for a book now which will content itself with making these preachers simply real, allowing them to make their own comments, out of the implications of their own lives, upon the preaching and the living of our own day.

B. C. C.

Syracuse, New York.

Contents

I

THE PREACHER WHO STIRRED UP
TROUBLE—ISAIAH

IN the long list of the books of the Bible, which most of us memorized as a part of our childhood training, there are seventeen items which are classified as Prophets. We say their names through, more or less glibly; occasionally we start into one of these books with a desperate resolution to see what it is all about, only to be discouraged by the difficulties which confront our most attentive reading. We realize that their contents must be bound up somewhere in the unified message of the Bible, and we have a dim feeling that by some mysterious process these books accomplished a preparation for Jesus.

But they make such disheartening reading, because each book seems to be an inextricable mixture of narrative, historical background, impassioned exhortations, wild visions, and interruptions of one kind or another. These varied parts are not set off from one another by punctuation or typography; no quotation marks warn us of a change in conversation; the chapters seem like hopelessly illogical divisions, and the verses have no slightest justification in fact. The language is over-ornate and flowery, and we grow scornful of its exuberant extravagance.

Of course, we should be warned at the outset that these Prophets are not books, but people. Prophets are not ideas or subjects or themes, but men. These stories and rebukes and retorts and adventures, are all strands in the tapestry of human life. These are the traces left by the greatest religious figures in the race which produced Jesus. They happen to be preserved in the precious medium of literature rather than in the beauties of art or the interesting shelves of a museum of relics. But this must not delude us into believing that Isaiah is a book. Isaiah is a man.

If such stress upon an obvious fact seems fantastic, observe how few people ever think of these names as representing an intensely interesting galaxy of men. Observe how many discussions have treated them as books and how few have portrayed them as men. Much of the literature which we find under their names expresses their ideas. But even this literature is not in the form of writing. It is preaching. That it got itself written later has no bearing on the matter at all. These men are not authors. They are preachers. These ideas were not spun out by the slow leisurely process of silk-worm webbing, in a carefully controlled study temperature. Instead, these phrases leaped like hot flames out of the indignant conflagrations of outraged souls. These sentences were not handled and polished and turned and shaped and decked by the watchful skill of a quiet craftsman. They were hammered together to meet a sudden occasion, and their rough jointures betray them. The interplay of voice upon voice must be heard, the intuitive changes in tone and shifts of pace in utterance must be appreciated, the shuffling, listening, angry, cowardly crowds must be imagined, the interjected comments must be supplied, the scene of the preaching must be recreated in the mind, the history of the mood must be explored, if the story of these prophets is to be understood.

A *book* bears within itself its complete justification,—explaining itself and creating its own background. But *these fragments* ripped out of the material of life are totally meaningless as such. They must be surrounded by the efforts of those who deem the task worth while. So throughout

this series of portraits, we shall dare to call these men "preachers," rather than "prophets," for preachers they really were, and the word prophet, unaided, lifts them too far out of the pleasant region of our acquaintance.

The years have made their changes in the meaning of the word "prophet." As we hear it now, we think of one who predicts the nature of coming events. A prophet foretells, prognosticates, the weather, or the course of business, or the price of grain, or our own future fate. But years ago, when these preachers were first called prophets, the word bore no such significance. A prophet was a forth-teller, a representative, an advocate for one who could not speak for himself. These prophets spoke for God, as His mouthpiece among men.

When Moses began his great mission of emancipation, his limitations immediately became apparent. He could not speak well in public. He could arrange, he could plan, he could confer, he could dare, he could direct, but he could not orate. He confessed his shortcoming to God, and suggested that this lack probably made him ineligible for the work. But God promised to supply a mouthpiece for him. He appointed Aaron to speak the words for Moses. When Moses had some proclamation to make, he spoke the words to Aaron, and Aaron

lifted up his voice and passed the word on, un-
falteringly and effectively, to the people. Aaron√
was Moses' prophet. He did not predict, he proclaimed. He did not foretell,—he did forth-tell.
This is the only true meaning of the word in Biblical vocabulary. And because, when we want to
mean that, we say not " prophet " but " preacher,"
this book is to be made up of the Portraits of
twelve Preachers.

Of course, occasionally one of these preachers,
forced by the circumstances of his work, will be
found enforcing his point by describing what he
thinks will happen if people do not take his advice.
But this is not predicting. This is the essence of
preaching. There are even traces of the expectation of Christ's coming duly outlined in the hopes
of these preachers. And this wistful pointing
toward the day of Messiah's coming is, of course,
a beautiful link between the Old and the New
Testaments. But this expression of the Messianic
hope was only a part of the effort on behalf of
Jesus which these preachers made. They spent so
little time in merely pointing. They spent so much
more time in actually making the road, over which
his royal feet must travel—the road of true ideas,
the road of holy moods, the road of sincere morals,
the road of glorifying love for God and men. This

was their mission. True, they did love his appearing. And their love for its promise found its way into words often. But they were not satisfied merely to gaze in his general direction. They were not content to describe the place and the circumstances in which they hoped he would come. They prepared the way. They made his paths straight. They exalted the valleys and leveled off the hills. When he came, he paid tribute to their services. They were his forerunners.

In no single prophet are all these introductory considerations more obvious than in Isaiah. To the average Christian, Isaiah is a book of sixty-six chapters, containing a variety of writings, including certain bold predictions which indicate with miraculous accuracy the coming of Jesus. It may surprise us to know that to his contemporaries, Isaiah was a preacher, possessing unusual eloquence, lashing his people for their sins, and taking delight in stirring them up out of their lethargy into fresh outbursts of furious pugnacity.

Of course, Isaiah was a preacher and not a book. Some of the most interesting paragraphs in the account are devoted to vivid episodes of his thrilling adventures. A glorious story tells us with wealth of detail the events leading up to his call to be a prophet.

King Uzziah has just died. This young man, Isaiah, city-bred, nobly-born, carefully-trained, highly-destined, had loved and honoured Uzziah. He is in the temple mourning his death. The presence of God suddenly overwhelms him, the voice of God addresses him, the holiness of God shames him, the redemption of God cleanses him, the challenge of God claims him, and he says, "Here am I."

Chapter upon chapter follows, capturing for the ages the otherwise vanished, but now deathless eloquence of this master of human speech. We see the crowds sway before his denunciation, we watch kings blanch at his scathing rebukes, we see armies grow courageous under his discipline, we watch a heathen host retreat before his wrath and faith. We watch the balances of the world's destiny sway back and forth as he sets the weights of his influence. For three long reigns, he rules the fate of Judah, and with it the fate of the world. By the sheer moral power of his preaching, he makes the policies of his epoch.

Uzziah died while Isaiah was only a boy, but the good king had left an example of glorious achievement which cried out for emulation. Jotham became sovereign, after ruling for years in his father's behalf, while Uzziah slowly yielded to the inroads of leprosy. Like a weak echo, Jotham sent back the influences of Uzziah's life, ruling in peace for sixteen years.

Then came Ahaz, his son, violently overthrowing all the record of those patient efforts. The House of the Lord was defiled, Baal was worshipped in Jerusalem, and human sacrifices became the climax-rite of pagan worship in the holy city, patterned after the Phœnician orgies. Assyria arose like an avenging fate and invaded the land.

Ahaz yielded at last to death, and Hezekiah became king. Good in every intention, but weak in faith and in execution, he needed the steadying strength which Isaiah alone seemed able to supply. So Isaiah became his shield and buckler, warding off the tragic debacle which would have been his fate had he been left alone. With all these kings, Isaiah acted as counsellor on the Lord's behalf. Often spurned, often disobeyed, he said his say so that all could hear, and each new year brought a greater national confidence in the integrity of his purposes and the courage of his faith and the wisdom of his pious statesmanship.

Dealing with world events as an advisor of monarchs, Isaiah found it necessary to outline occasionally the course of events as he foresaw it. But the content of his predictions is insignificant compared with the startling volume of his protests against the iniquity and cowardice of his people. He gladly left off foretelling without a qualm, and turned to a fearless forth-telling, while he proclaimed to his people how vile they looked in the eyes of God. With scathing boldness he described the hideous injustice of the prevailing distribution of wealth, the love of baubles, the frantic indulgence in luxurious vice, the frightful orgies of drunkenness which characterized the conscience-less existence of the city. Under his stinging whip-lash, the whole nation cringed, as he forced wanton pleasure to hide in shame.

Yet when he died and men looked back over the events of his life, they recalled not his eloquence nor his denunciations. They remembered him as a preacher who was always stirring them up when they wanted to be let alone. He kept saying, " War, war, war," when all they wanted was a chance to make a good bargain for peace. He would not let them enjoy their comforts, he would not let them take their ease. He kept whipping them up into furies, year after year, in the name of the Lord. He was the preacher who stirred up trouble.

This note first emerged from his preaching while Ahaz reigned. The northern kingdom, Israel, was mobilizing for an ambitious attack upon Jerusalem. News of the preparations was borne to the people of Judah. Their army was small, their border was difficult to defend, they were busy about other things, but, of course, they could not avoid this attack. So they fell to planning and arming. But someone suggested an easier way out. Assyria was near by. The allies of the northern kingdom included the rival nation, Syria. If the Judæans could only convince Assyria that the planned attack was a veiled threat upon Assyrian power, and that if Judah were conquered Assyria would be the next to suffer, then the Assyrian army would be placed at their disposal and the problem of defense would be solved.

The plan was tried, the negotiations were begun. Tiglath-Pileser, king of Assyria, consented. He would bring his magnificent army to the defense of Jerusalem, all his engines of war would repel the attack. Of course, he would have to have some tribute money as a reward, and, of course, the Assyrian gods would demand a place in the temple of Jehovah, but he would fight their war for them. When Isaiah heard of the terms, he shouted in rage at the threatened bargain. He knew that the years would make his people slaves under the pressure of the payments, he knew that the conquering army of Assyria could take anything from its tiny ally once the victory had been won, and he knew what would happen to the true faith once these pagan gods were welcomed. He fought the issue before the king, but the king was adamant. He pursued the monarch in his intensity, pleading with him as he traveled about inspecting the preparations for the battle. At the water-works, he made his last request. Ahaz insisted on carrying out the contract with Assyria.

Then Isaiah fearlessly took the matter to the people. He knew that Judah could win alone. He knew that this alliance would mean bondage. He knew that Jehovah could not smile upon this yoke of partnership with Tiglath-Pileser. But the people smiled at his fury, referred him to the king, and let the scheme work out. The Assyrians came, they beat back the northern foes, they set their price, they put up their shrines in the sacred places, they despoiled the Temple of the most High, and thereafter Judah struggled hopelessly, a pawn in the game of imperial tradings and military ambitions.

When Hezekiah mounted the throne, Egypt was rising in new power. Great Pharaohs had built for world conquests. The might of Assyria was challenged. Judah was forced to choose. Should the king renew his old allegiance with Assyria, or should he shift to greet the new conquerors from Egypt? If Isaiah had been given the choice between one alliance or none, he would have chosen none. But forced to choose between the old contract, and a new one that ventured into unknown possibilities of peril, he chose, and passionately advocated, the side of Assyria. For a long time Hezekiah wavered, while Isaiah pleaded and wept and prayed and threatened and stormed and wooed. At last the prophet had his way, the old compact was renewed. But only after he had walked the streets of Jerusalem naked and sad, to bring home to the people the shame and sorrow of their slavery if they should happen to choose the wrong rival in the desperate game with death.

Sargon, King of Assyria, beat back the Egyptians in a great battle on the field of Raphia, and the kingdom of Judah bowed at last to the political acumen and the holy earnestness of their bothersome, restless prophet.

The climax of Isaiah's career came late in the reign of Hezekiah. Sennacherib, the new king of Assyria, had attacked Judah, gained the promise of new and greater tribute from Hezekiah, and had camped outside the walls of Jerusalem under strict pledge that he would spare the city from suffering.

Hezekiah evidently did not trust him, for he moved stealthily out of Jerusalem to Lachish, where he would be safe. Suddenly Sennacherib violated every promise, and with fiendish glee started to ruin Judah's fair capital. He claimed that rumours had informed him of Hezekiah's treacherous advances to the king of Egypt, in order to summon their army to help against the Assyrians. The tale was a lie, but it served as a good excuse, and the Assyrians leaped to their cruel task.

In this crisis, all eyes turned toward Isaiah, now an old man. Hezekiah could do nothing. Defense was unthinkable. The Assyrians were a host that swarmed round the city walls. Judah's little army was a handful. Hezekiah felt that he must submit. He turned to Isaiah, and asked for word from on high. The preacher spoke on God's behalf:

"Do not surrender. Keep up your courage. I shall send a blast upon Sennacherib, and he shall hear a rumour and return to his own land, and I will cause him to fall by the sword in his own land."

Hezekiah was astounded. He knew that the Assyrians boasted one of the great military machines of the world. He knew that they had already taken captive forty-six of Hezekiah's strong cities, and that they had enslaved 200,000 of his people. He knew that they were boasting that they had him now shut up like a caged bird in Jerusalem. But Isaiah was certain and would not be dissuaded. The king believed him. Isaiah caught upon the first symptom of his faith, and with a voice that broke with emotion, said, " The Lord will turn aside the Assyrians. They shall not harm you. They shall never send so much as a single arrow against your wall."

" Then an angel of the Lord went forth and smote in the camp of the Assyrians, a hundred and fourscore and five thousand." Explain it as you will, doubt it if you must, the record appears not only in the narratives of Judah, but on the tablets of Assyrian history as well. And whatever else you may claim, it is still a fact that Jerusalem was spared. Years afterward, Sennacherib died upon his own sword in his own land. God had justified His preacher. Hezekiah was delivered from his cage. The people were preserved from death. In some way or other, the Lord did provide.

It was Isaiah's unpleasant duty to be consistently hurling himself against any tempting compromise, and continually stirring up the people to the pitch of self-sacrificial warfare. It was a hard life. When people pleaded to be left alone, with their easy bargains and their modest hopes, he was forced to rally them to the attack. When smiling sovereigns offered to protect them for a price, Isaiah scorned the proffered alliance and besought Judah to fight alone, with God.

His challenge rings out like a battle-cry over religion today. Compromise is so easy. The world looks so innocent and helpful. Tact is such a pleasant thing. There is so tiny a line of demarcation between skilful teaching, and the dishonesty of compromise. We want to get along well with people. We hesitate to hurt feelings and to make enemies. We enjoy peace and ease, and the price seems so little. We do not care to injure people's sensibilities by undue affirmation. We want to be nice.

We are cowards! Beware when all men speak well of you. We are submitting to the secret and diabolical infiltration of the enemy. We need to feel the whip-lash of an Isaiah's fury. Make no alliance with the Mammon of unrighteousness. If you are true and brave and ready, you need not fear. God will deliver you.

> "It may not be my way,
> It may not be thy way,
> But yet in his own way,
> The Lord will provide."

II

THE PREACHER WHO NEVER WENT TO SCHOOL—AMOS

NICHOLAS MURRAY BUTLER, President of Columbia University, has recently diagnosed our national ills, as is his custom, in his annual report to Columbia's Board of Trustees. He has discovered several alarming new symptoms. We are suffering, he avers, from the results of an uneducated ministry. Standards of eligibility for the Protestant pulpit are pitiably low, and standards of salary have dropped to the level of the man-quality. Ordination councils are farces, theological preparation is careless and poorly devised, men with less than high school training have obtained the degree of Doctor of Divinity and been placed in influential pulpits only because they seem to possess that gift of doubtful value—the gift of speech. As a general result, we have turned loose upon our innocent congregations a great flood of half-educated, opinionated, skill-less, confident bunglers, who lack the technique of properly moulding public opinion, and who, when they do attempt it, poison the general mind with archaic superstitions and the fears of gross ignorance.

Of course, President Butler knows how to cure this disease. He would favour a nation-wide demand for a better-trained ministry. He would insist upon certain well-defined professional requirements such as now apply to the medical world. He would silence every pulpit orator who cannot claim the credentials of a recognized theological seminary. He would make sure that certain courses in general culture, in scientific methods and achievements, in the specific practice of the preaching art, were included in the divinity school curriculum. Thus would he prevent the imposition of half-baked, ill-considered, radical and destructive ideas from the pulpit upon the people, in the name of the Christian religion.

His ideal is a reasonable one, and it finds its echo in thousands of minds. Certainly the things of religion are complicated enough at best. Philosophy, comparative religion, psychology of the individual and psychology of the crowd, archæology, Hebrew and Greek, Biblical history, Church history, Christian doctrine, sociology, economics, general science, biology,—these cannot be mastered in

a day, nor in a short course by correspondence. So
close is the approach to the popular mind which
the successful popular preacher achieves, that we
hesitate to entrust the transaction to an individual
who has yielded to no control in his preparation
and is under no control in his ministry. We want
men to be pronounced fairly safe before we can
consent to their occupying the throne of oratory.
We feel that we have a right to demand that our
minds be spared from the boresome preachments
of boors who have never known the backgrounds
of literature, possess no cultured skill in words, and
have no steady constructive program of thinking
and planning. These untrained men seem to mani-
fest a fiendish delight in tearing things down.
They attack the *status quo* with such zest. They
are so tactless, so bull-headed, so impolite. We
think we know what Dr. Butler is talking about
when he fulminates against an uneducated ministry.
Surely church people do deserve a happier fate than
is theirs. Surely they have a right to ask for some
assurance that their preachers will be gentlemen,
and scholars, and builders in the tasks of the
Church and the community.

So Christians in general, while feeling that Dr.
Butler might have added to his list of ills, an irreligious education, as well as an uneducated religion,

are inclined to agree with him in his general conviction. If we insist upon safe, dependable, cultured, trained, constructive teachers, and doctors, and lawyers—then we have the right to demand such preachers.

Exactly such talk was current in Jerusalem, and in Judah and Israel generally, eight hundred years before Christ. But it had become mellow and confident with years of repetition and reassertion, until it had become an assumed point in the mind of the official church. If a man wanted to become a priest, there were certain authorized and specific courses of training which were outlined. If a man felt called to be a prophet, he was not on this account and in that moment a prophet. The call was regarded as an interesting indication of a remote possibility. He did not at once begin to prophesy. The idea was absurd. First, he submitted an account of his family history, with particular attention to the members of his past generations who had shown some disposition for religious things. Then he outlined the circumstances of his call, the situation which provoked it, his moods and reactions toward the sacred summons. Then he stated the reasons why he was certain that God had made a formal and recognizable demand upon his life.

If these two matters could be satisfactorily explained, he might enter his name on the list of candidates for the school of the prophets, where the traditional forms of prophecy might be studied, the literary style of the various epochs discussed, the theological trends and developments traced from generation to generation, and the great personal figures examined for their strengths and their faults, their methods and their messages.

The slow, relentless progress of the truth of God, "broadening from precedent to precedent," might be observed in a careful course on the history of Judah and Israel. The work of the prophet was contrasted with the offices of the priest. The lines of demarcation were carefully drawn. Perhaps there was added a lecture course on "How to Get Along Well with People," embracing such related themes as "The Folly of Rubbing People the Wrong Way," "How to Influence the King toward the Truth," "The Value of Tact to a Prophet," and other elements of successful salesmanship as applied to promoting the prophetic idea. When the stipulated requirements were fulfilled, the diplomas were issued, "by the authority of the State and the Church and the School," and the candidate became a fledgling prophet. He might then address himself to the people, who would trust him, not

because he told the truth or told it well, but because he was properly and completely certified
and guaranteed.

Bethel was swarming with religious devotees.
It was the day of the great feast. For miles
around, the country had emptied itself into the
templed city for the happy exercise of a public
religious festival. The priests were busy at their
work, carrying through the impressive ritual of the
ancient and beautiful forms. Prophets were speaking to eager worshippers, saying the things they
had been taught to say in the skilful ways which
the schools had taught them. The people were
comfortably worshipping and listening, well-clad,
bejewelled, fat and prosperous, nodding their heads
in careful and conservative approval, thankful for
the rounded sentences from cultured, tactful, gen-
tlemanly preachers who had passed the tests of an
educated ministry. The Nicholas Murray Butlers
of Israel had gained their way. Religion was
hermetically protected from the half-wits now.
The only way one could preach was by submitting
oneself to the training of the Church and after that
training had been completed one had only one way
to preach and that was the tamed, correct way.
Over you floated the little banners which certified

your loyalty to the Church and to the country and
to the king.

But look! The crowds are stirring uneasily. A
rumour is leaping from lip to lip. Some madman
has come to town, shouting mad things and claiming to be a prophet. He will not be silenced. He
raves like a fool.

Who is he? Amos, is his name. Amos? Amos?
We know no prophet by the name of Amos. What
was his school? What is his town? Who was his
father? Who taught him? When was he called to
prophesy? Where are his diplomas?

No one knows his father. He has admitted that
there is no strain of prophet-blood in his veins. He
says that he comes from Tekoa. You remember
that little God-forsaken, barren village up on the
edge of the desert hills! When we ask him his
trade, he points to his garments and says, " You
can see that I am a herdsman." And once he admitted that he had been a sycamore-dresser, earn-
ing his living by plucking those poor, forlorn,
flavourless sycamore buds into ripeness so that he
might sell the figs to poor folk in his neighbour-
hood. He says (think of this from a prophet!)
that he has never been to school!

Never been to school? Well, of course, that dis-
poses of him. If he wants to be a prophet, he

knows the necessary steps. If he feels the call, let him submit himself to the examiners, and take the prescribed tests. Have we reached the place where we must listen to the babblings of any fool who claims to speak in the name of the Lord? Very probably, if we deigned to listen, we should find him speaking some outlandish, slangy tongue, railing against everything that is, and perhaps even assailing the king. But, of course, we shall not listen. That is what we have seminaries for, to train prophets. We know a prophet when we see one. We ask for his official credentials. If he has none, then he is no prophet.

But here he is now, stalking down the main street unconcerned, a great mob moiling around him. He is stopping. They are lifting him up upon some steps. He is speaking. It is a weird vocabulary he is using. We told you so. And yet he speaks well. His voice is not a trained voice. See those awkward gestures. No one has coached him. And see those uncontrolled sobs, watch the tears course down his dusty cheeks. What is that he is saying?

"Thus saith Jehovah;—For three transgressions of Damascus, yea for four, I will not turn away the punishment thereof, because they have threshed Gilead with their instruments of iron."

A murmur of assent sweeps over the crowd. Prophet or no prophet, he is right about that. The heartless cruelty of Damascus has become a by-word with us. Damascus deserves punishment. Let us listen to him for a moment.

"Thus saith Jehovah; For three transgressions of Edom, yea for four, I will not turn away the punishment thereof, because he did pursue his brother with the sword and did cut off all pity."

The crowd's murmur becomes a united mumble of approval. We know Edom—Edom did violate every friendly contract, and treacherously betray her brothers. Go on, Amos, you are right!

"Thus saith Jehovah; For three transgressions of the children of Ammon, yea for four, I will not turn away the punishment thereof, because they have ripped up the women with child of Gilead, that they may enlarge their border."

There are voices that rise in shouts of agreement. People in the crowd are recalling the news of that awful cruelty, when lust for power made fiends out of the army of Ammon, and wrote a record of dreadful pain in the blood of women and unborn babies. Go on, Amos! More truth!

"Thus saith Jehovah; For three transgressions of Moab, yea for four, I will not turn away the punishment thereof, because he burned the bones of the king of Edom into lime."

Cheers rise on every lip. The crowd has been completely won. This brave man is telling them tremendous truths. There has not been written in this generation a more wanton disgrace than this infamous deed of Moab. There could be no possible excuse for this indignity to the conquered king's body. God has a right to punish them. We are with you, Amos! Go on!

" Thus saith Jehovah; For three transgressions of Judah, yea for four, I will not turn away the punishment thereof, because they have rejected the law of Jehovah, and have not kept his statutes, and their lies have caused them to err after which their fathers did walk. But I will send a fire upon Judah, and shall devour the palaces of Jerusalem."

The crowd goes mad in a tumult of enthusiasm. Judah is our neighbour on the south—proud, cynical rival of ours. Judah is built around Jerusalem, always boasting about Jerusalem, always scorning her neighbours, always claiming the special blessing and benediction of Jehovah. But we know that they have sinned sorely against God, and that they have deserted Jehovah whose name they mouth so often. And now this brave man says that Judah will be destroyed, that the palaces of Jerusalem will be ruined in the fire. He speaks the truth. We do not care about his birthplace. We do not care about his schooling. He is right. He is brave. He knows the mind of God. Go on, Amos! More! More! More!

The wild storm of approval mounts and dies away, and the voice of the prophet speaks again:

"Thus saith Jehovah; For three transgressions of Israel," (Israel? Israel? That means us!) "For three transgressions of Israel, yea for four, I will not turn away the punishment thereof, because they have sold the righteous for silver and the needy for a pair of shoes, they that pant after the dust of the earth on the head of the poor and turn aside the way of the meek; and a man and his father go unto the same maiden to profane my holy name, and they lay themselves down beside every altar upon clothes taken in pledge and in the house of their God they drink the wine of such as have been fined."

The cheering, jeering, maddened mob is silent now. Their pride has been turned upon themselves. They have wildly acclaimed the judgments pronounced upon their guilty neighbours. Now they are cowed by the promised destruction of their own guilty selves. They had trained the prophets. But their prophets had never talked to them like

that, had never made them feel like that. This bold
man had lashed them, and cursed them, and puri-
fied them, in the name of God. This preaching
had overwhelmed them.

Of course, no one learns to preach like that in
the schools. The schools teach you how it should
be done by showing you how it has been done.
That is the trouble with the schools. The only
fault with the old way is that it is old. And
because it is old it has less chance to make its
own way vividly into minds. It has been tried
too often before.

Schools give you the well-tested methods of the
successful men in the past centuries. Schools in-
troduce you to the classic examples of oratorical
achievement. Schools formulate the preaching of
the past into rules, " Introduction, text, points—
one, two, three, four—peroration." Schools tell
you what is correct homiletically. Schools seldom
stimulate toward the untried way, the novel approach, the violently different message. No school
would have encouraged Amos to begin his vivid
swing around the circle of Israel's neighbours,
whipping the crowd to outbursts of self-complaisant
boasting, until at last he pinned the judgments of
God down into their own quivering flesh and left
them in agony and contrition. It had never been

done before. It could not work. But it did work. Just because it had never been done before. The prophets never talked like that. That is the great risk of insisting upon standards of teaching for prophets. You get standardized prophets. And prophecy is the one place in the world where standardization is fatal as a method. Jesus " spoke as one having authority, not as the scribes." What a comment on the scribes—of his day—and of ours!

Of course, Amos never learned this bitter, terrifying frankness in the schools. This fierce, honest cataloguing of sins is not the product of careful culture. When he pilloried Israel, he did not select fair words. They sold human beings for silver and shoes, he said, and those who listened blushed at their social infamy. Father and son sought the same maiden to profane her, he said. They hung their heads at their flamboyant immoralities. The clothes and the wine of the poor are seized by the rich for a pledge, and are used in the Temple for the hypocrisy of worship, he charged. Soft hands touched lovely fabrics as he spoke, and shamed minds wished that they had not chosen these garments for this particular feast day. This direct aim, this leveled forefinger of recrimination, this deliberate discomfiture of a congregation—these things are not taught in the schools. They are

poor psychology. You must not offend. People
may not want to come again. The schools teach
you to be diplomatic, to be tactful, to be smooth
and successful, to give no offense, to hurt no feelings. The schools teach you to be such a skilful
pedagogue that you succeed in teaching your truth
by slow degrees through a series of years, while
your pupils are not aware of your intention, and so
no one is afraid. But the schools scorn the rude,
rough eloquence of a plumb-line laid brutally
against a wall, while a demand is made that the
wall be demolished and a new, straight one be built
from the very foundation.

Of course, Amos had not learned his poignant
social sympathy, his shameless tears and sobs, in
the schools. Schools teach you to be ashamed of
inartistic emotion. Hebrew and Greek are excel-
lent, but they do have a way of lifting one out of
the miseries of a vernacular world, and blunting
the edge of compassion. The scholar's sanctum
makes the scholar feel somewhat distinct from the
sordid suffering of commonplace people on the
streets. Amos feels their wrongs because he does
come directly out of them, and he is about to go
directly back into them. Society and inequality
are not abstractions to him. His own cloak has
been seized. He has touched shameless hungry

women on the streets. His voice shakes, his body
writhes with passion, his eyes flood with tears. He
does not care. He has not been to the school of
the prophets where they might have taught him
how to control these things.

Of course, Amos has not learned this fearless
defiance of the king in the schools. When he
names the king, and hurls invectives and threats
upon him, he is violating the safe dictates of culture. It is a well-trained, educated priest named
Amaziah who interrupts his wild tirade, to protest,
and when Amos will not stop, Amaziah hurries
away to tell the king about this absurd babbler,
who will not listen to reason. Schools are loyal.
Schools protect the *status quo*. Schools bask in
the sunshine of royal favour. Schools encourage
in their progeny that care for Alma Mater that
makes one ashamed of bringing a blush of shame
to her fair cheeks. And, of course, treason would
break her heart.

Amos had not gone to school. It was some
disadvantage to him, no doubt. But at least he
preached in a new way, and he named sins with a
new frankness, and he wept with a new sincerity
of human sympathy, and he threatened with a new
boldness. And the real fools were the people who
spurned him because he had never been to school.

His ministry is no apology for general ignorance. His methods are not to be taken as an indictment of an educated ministry. In this, I am Pharisee of the Pharisees. The finest faculties of the world have poured out their treasures at my feet and have given me all that they had. But I hope I know enough to save me from demanding that people pay attention to me merely because I have studied so long. And I hope I know enough to refuse to close my mind to a message merely because it is not prefaced with a convincing citation of degrees.

I pray to be delivered from that state of mind which rejects Keats because he was a druggist's apprentice; which sniffs at Whitman because his yawp was barbaric; which discounts Luther because his home was humble; which scorns Wesley because he left the English Establishment; which spurns Francis E. Clark and his Christian Endeavour Society because he had taken no course in modern education; which rejects Billy Sunday because when he prays he says uncouth things to God; which refuses to consider Burbank's ideas because he happens to be an expert in botany instead of an expert in religion (expert in religion? what is that?); which smiles superciliously at Jesus because the garments on his shoulders are dusty with carpenter-shop débris, and his speech smacks of Nazareth, and which dismisses Amos because he never went to school. From this ultimate snobbery, good Lord, deliver us!

If Amos teaches us anything, he teaches us not to trust in training for all truth, and not to spurn rude truth merely because it is rude.

Amos, who " towers in the distance like an earth-born Atlas—such a man, in such an historical position, standing on the confines of light and darkness, like day on the misty mountain-tops,"—Amos, who " is one of the most wonderful appearances in the history of the human spirit "—Amos—never went to school!

III

THE PREACHER WHOSE HEART WAS BROKEN—HOSEA

TO the matter-of-fact mind, a landscape is a landscape, whoever happens to be looking at it. Compounded of certain measurable proportions of green and brown, of light and shadow, it exists in itself, and the distinctions between individual reactions to it seem like fanciful vagaries.

> "A primrose by a river's brim
> A yellow primrose was to him,
> And it was nothing more."

It is for this reason that the matter-of-fact mind deserves on occasion to confront two such seers as Amos and Hosea, and to observe what happens to them as they view the same landscape.

Amos looks out over Israel and sees nothing but the background for the vast drama of God's wrath with the sons of men. These rocky crevices are only waiting for the fierce lurid light of God's lightning, when His patience is exhausted. These towns are soon to be shaken into dust by the shattering force of God's cataclysm, or ground into ruin before the chariot-wheels of God's avengers. These groves of trees are drooping already in anticipation of the blight and the drought which will come upon them as the signs of God's anger. The only beauty that exists in the realm of nature is the beauty of the stars—signs of the imperturbable, invincible, inviolable, implacable justice of a God who hates sin wherever He sees it.

Hosea views the same landscape. But he broods over it with the tenderness of a poet-lover, glorifying the scene with his pattern of lovely words. The vines trail their graceful tendrils over the rocks; the olive tree flutters its leaves under the noonday sun; the first ripe fig of the fig tree in her first season is a symbol of promise; the scent of Lebanon reaches him on the wings of the summer breeze. Smoke rises in gray wisps from happy dwellings, doves fly up in sudden, frightened confusion and then wheel into orderly ranks of flight; the clods give forth the pungent odour of the spring planting; the heifer treads out the corn upon the threshing-floor; the smiling driver feeds his oxen as they pause in their yokes. The same landscape —but a new pair of eyes.

Thus Amos looked out upon a universe and saw

a God of law. Hosea, in the same universe, saw a
God of love. Both saw the same God. Both were
right. And both were needed for the truth.

Amos comes storming down out of the country,
his soul writhing in disgust at the overweening sins
of the cities. Rich garments of costly fabrics,
careless selfishness, formal ritual in worship, im-
morality in fleshly lusts, the great gulf fixed between rich and poor—these things oppress and
dismay him. He shouts out his protest on a feast
day in Bethel, mows down his victims with the
fierce invective of his crude oratory, shows them
their sins as ghastly insults to a righteous God, and
leaves them heart-sick at their hopeless estrange-
ment from Jehovah. They have lived too sordidly,
they have spent too wildly, they have oppressed too
fiercely and too long—they cannot expect forgiveness. God has endured too much, God has tried
too often, God has judged too righteously—He
cannot win them back. " You alone have I known
of all the families of the earth; therefore will I
visit upon you all your iniquities."

Contrast all this with Hosea, son of Beeri, who
began life in the household of a priest, and bore a
name which meant " Salvation." Early his poet-
soul brought him those indescribable delights and
those unavoidable tortures which are the natural in-

heritance of all lovers of beauty. Dedicated to the Lord, he tried to conform his will to God's purposes, and God led him through his youth, clearly and surely.

As a young man, his love found its shrine in a woman's heart. Gomer was her name. He waited until he was sure of God's will. When he felt that the divine consent had been given, Hosea married his beloved, and the halcyon days of a poet's love began. Young, and happy, and beautiful, they found the summit of joy together. Yet like an undertone of ominous trouble beneath the light melody of their love, the sense of Israel's doom was ever in their minds. When their firstborn son was named, Hosea called him Jezreel, " the doom of the house of Israel," so that all who heard the name might remember Jehovah, and the quarrel which He had with His people.

How the first doubt came to his trusting heart we cannot tell. Perhaps some gossiping tongue passed on the tale indirectly until it reached his ears. Perhaps some furtive writing betrayed his wife's wicked plans, and showed him her unfaithfulness. Perhaps he happened upon her once surrounded by the signs of her treachery, and he drew back in surprise, unable to credit the evidence of his senses. This we know,—that when two years had passed, and a new baby-girl was born, Hosea's heart was bowed down with an awful certainty, and he named her "Lo-Ruhamah," "No-Pity," for Gomer, his wife, had shown him no pity, and he could not love this little girl as a father should.

The days passed in tragic sombre procession, each with its dark evidence of wrong-doing. The nights were haunted with fears and misgivings. Gossip swirled round them, his household was known in the city for its shame, people pointed to his children and whispered bitter things, he wept upon his bed, and bowed his head before this terrible fate which God had decreed for him. Gomer flaunted her sin and defied him. A third child was born, another boy. By this time his tormented mind left him no chance for doubt. He knew that the worst was the truth. All his mad imaginings were justified. The scandal was revealed. His wife had betrayed him. And he named the baby "Lo-Ammi," "He is no son of mine."

Then the break, which had been inevitable, came. The foolish pretence of love and respect and faithfulness became impossible. The city murmured about his disgrace. She did not care for his pleas, she had no heart for the children, she had trampled upon his love like a flower in the dust. She cursed his devotion, raved against his tenderness, and in the end, she left him to find her satisfaction in the maddening lust of her sin, while he did what he could to keep a home for his poor, motherless brood.

Out upon the streets she swaggered, to taste the full fruit of her choice. Ties of decency bound her no longer. The months had their wasting way with her. Her face grew haggard, her eyes burned like glowing coals of terrible desire, her hands were like the talons of a bird of prey. She sold herself to men, as they approached her. Down the levels of life she descended. And soon she was a slave, utterly degraded, utterly despised.

Meanwhile Hosea had done his best for the three children. How he managed, we have no definite hint. What happened to his fair dreams of prophetic power and of priestly privilege? What sordid reflections intruded upon his philosophy? We can only guess. Did he tell the three babies about their mother, and teach them to pray for her as they knelt by him at bed-time? Or did he shield her behind a merciful silence, and parry their questions with skilful evasions? There is no answer to these questions.

But, one day, when the years had passed, Hosea walked the streets of the city, his mind intent on other things. Time had been merciful enough to close up the gaping wound in the heart of him and to silence his pain. He had almost succeeded in rebuilding his life without her. Suddenly, he glances up and sees her, crouching there on the street-corner. Vile men swagger around her. Raucous voices taunt her. A slave-driver calls for bids on her flesh.

Hosea cringes as if he had been lashed with a whip. He tries to turn aside, but something within him prevents. He sees her eyes, he watches her. He listens while offers are made and sums are named for her possession. Bids vie with bids. The hammer is about to fall—the last bid has been entered—the transaction is closed.

No! Not yet! Hosea lifts his voice. He names a price far higher than the rest. Men eye him with suspicion. The master of the sale gapes at him. She looks up from her shame. He steps forward, empties his purse, and turns his eyes upon this woman whom he has bought.

All the compassion of his love leaps to enfold her. He has forgotten her sin, he has forgiven her shame. The days when he pleaded with her, the nights when she sneered at him, these are all erased from his mind. He does not see her rags, nor her parchment-cheeks—he does not notice her bedraggled hair nor her eyes with their dull blaze. He only knows that he loves her and pities her and receives her unto himself. To him she is once again the beautiful beloved of his boyhood dreams, the lovely bride of the long ago. He lifts her to her feet, covers her with caresses, woos her with affection, and bids her come back with him to be the queen of his life.

> *" Weeping blinding tears*
> *I took her to myself, and paid the price*
> *(Strange contrast to the dowry of her youth*
> *When first I wooed her); and she came again*
> *To dwell beneath my roof."*

I have wondered often what he said to the three children that day when he brought this sobbing stranger woman home with him to be their mother. I have wondered what they talked about—these two—when the darkness closed in on them that first night, and they began life together anew. But in the midst of these conjectures, one thing is certain. The blinding beauty of a new revelation was breaking across Hosea's heart that day.

" God is like that," he was thinking. " When I stood there watching her cower before her oppressors, something swept over me. I cannot explain it. I did not think, I did not remember, I did not plan, I did not judge—I just loved her again and my soul waited in anguished hope that when she looked up into my eyes she would know and love me. That is what happens to God when He looks upon erring men. God is like that. For that one moment, when I was at my best, I was touching the garments of God's love. God is like that! "

What happened to his home is veiled in mystery. But what happened to his preaching is revealed in the wooing sympathy of his recorded sermons. His life began to glow with the beauty of this new message. He went everywhere, preaching always the infinite patient mercy of God. He saw Israel, torn and broken, crouching in the by-ways of earth, sin-stained and heart-sick. He saw God standing by, not condemning, not sentencing, not abhorring, but loving and forgiving and seeking. God waited in hope that Israel would look up and know Him and realize His love.

" We who know Jehovah," said Hosea, " must go to the people of Israel and speak home to their hearts." Precious, beautiful phrase. " Speak home to their hearts." Like the lover who spins his dreams in happy words while his beloved listens. We must woo them to come home to Him while He waits with the love-light in His eyes.

> " To seek and save the lost,
> Forgetful of my calling and my fame,
> To call thee mine and bring thee back to God
> Became the master-passion of my heart."

Amos had preached that God was law—righteous, terrible, impersonal law. Hosea preached that God was love—tender, patient, forgiving love. He had no time to solve the eternal paradox. He did not take time to contradict the tradition of Amos. He preached what he knew. Out of his preaching came that lovely strain of prophetic melody which deepened and sweetened through the centuries until it reached its beauteous climax in the wonderful love of Jesus, which led him to Calvary for the sake of a lost world. "Neither do I condemn thee—go and sin no more."

"Oh, the shame of it," said Amos, as he looked upon Israel's sin. "Oh, the pity of it," said Hosea, and the blessed work of God's redeeming love had begun.

Perhaps we are not quite satisfied with these emotional processes as contributing to theological conclusions. Most of us are suspicious of the revelations which come out of the hot cauldron of personal experiences. We prefer for our guidance the cool, steely truth of quiet, impersonal thought, or the logical finalities of a large structure of reasonable convictions. But we are wrong, thus to mistrust the immediate knowledge of our suffering hearts. There are some things which the mind cannot know until the heart teaches it the truth.

The finest lesson I ever had in charity, I learned as I rocked my baby boy through the hours of pain and hunger on a winter morning. The doctors had told us weeks before that he must have only a special kind of prepared milk. A blizzard had descended upon our city and had cut off ordinary communication. The streets were drifted deep with piles of snow, and sleds were stalled, after their drivers had battled for hours against impossible barriers. When we looked, in the morning, for the accustomed bottle of milk, no such supply was to be found.

This boy of ours was hungry, and he knew it, and he expressed himself in no uncertain terms. The company informed us by telephone that they would hurry the delivery as fast as possible, but that at best there would be several hours' delay. So I took my little son, and rocked him back and forth, while I crooned to him my heartfelt sympathy. He did not understand about the blizzard, he did not care for sympathy, these melodious excuses seemed like a mockery to him. He was hungry and evasions would not do.

But soon he cried himself off to sleep, and I rocked him quietly to keep him from waking. As he dreamed there upon my lap, the recollection of his hunger would intrude, and he would sob and whimper pitifully in his slumber. I watched him, suffered with him. And as I lulled him off some tears stole down my cheeks and dropped upon his tousled head. Poor, hungry little boy!

Then I thought of the thousands of babies in the squalid poverty of the world's want. I thought of young fathers who had to watch their babies die for lack of a little food. I thought of the sleepless nights and the tortured days as anguished little bodies withered away, and eyes glazed in hopeless suffering.

Soon the milkman came. It had only been a few hours of hunger and waiting, at most. But as we wakened him from his haunted slumber, and gave him good warm milk, I hurried away to send a gift to the hungry babies of the world. And as I hurried, I thought, "God is like that! When I feel as I do now, caught up in all the misery and all the contented laughter of all the little babies of the world, I am treading on the threshold of God's pity and God's love. God is like that!"

Several months later, we had to take this baby boy of ours to a hospital for a minor operation. I saw his little body go stiff and then sag limp under the influence of the anæsthetic. I watched them invade his little throat with gleaming steel. I picked him up and huddled him over my shoulder when they were done with him, while a nameless, wordless fear gripped my heart, as I watched the blood on his flower-like skin. Then they banished me, lest he awake and find me. For they would have to keep him in the hospital for several days, and they did not want him disturbed by home-recollections.

When a week had passed, they summoned us by telephone to come and claim him. All those intervening days we had not seen him. We had called at the hospital and had tiptoed near his ward, but they had kept us from him. Our household on the hill had seemed grimly quiet all week, for lack of him.

We waited in a lobby while they dressed him and wrapped him warmly for his journey home. We heard his voice behind the closed door, in a little chatter of excited expectation. Then his mother turned to me and whispered, " Oh, I wonder if he will know us." Our thoughts froze at the dreadful possibility. A whole week! Can it be that he has forgotten?

They carried out the little pink-blanketed bundle that was our boy. We waited in terrible anguish. They turned his face toward us. He looked. Then a smile lighted his eyes, and he lifted his hands toward us. He knew us! Our cheeks were wet with happy tears! He knew us! We hugged him to our hearts. He knew us!

And I thought, " God is like that! He is bending over every sinner in the world, forgetting everything else, just hoping against hope that when those eyes look up into His, there will be a smile of recognition." Look up, and smile back at God. He loves you.

When we are at our best, we are within seeing distance of the eternal mercy of God. Our brightness of affection and tenderness is but the shadow of God's life.

> " When I am dead, what I have felt so long
> My soul shall know in clearer, purer light—
> That when I loathed and hated, I was wrong—
> That when I loved and pitied I was right."

Shame and hate and abhorrence—they have their place in our hearts as we think of our own sins. But for others, pity. There is some hope of good in everyone—this is the invincible confidence of the Christian.

God is love,—merciful, patient, forgiving love. And Hosea, blinded by tears, glimpsed for the first time in the world, through his grief, the smile of God's forgiveness.

IV

THE PREACHER WHO PITIED THE
POOR—MICAH

MICAH is the preacher who may be best portrayed in terms of what he is not. He says nothing affirmative about himself. His contemporaries have left no slightest record of what he really was. We have as our materials for identification only the negatives and the contrasts of his life.

The resulting likeness is a silhouette. We can find no opportunity to reproduce Micah's features, the glint of his eye, the wave of his hair. But we can see him as a black mass outlined sharply against the background of his time. This shadow-portrait is made up out of the things which Micah was not. It develops into a very interesting and informing picture. It need not surprise us. I have seen daguerreotype profiles in old albums which were much more lifelike than are the prettified, retouched photos of our modern studios. There is such a thing as revealing too much to reveal anything real.

What do we know about heaven? Many, many things. If we take only the material provided in the Book of Revelation, we find page after page of rich description all relating directly to life after death. Gorgeous symbols are poured out before us like treasures from the jewel-boxes of an oriental monarch; rich fabrics of dream-language are displayed as we watch with wondering eyes. The very sounds of heaven are caught and held for us in the mystic syllables which come from the glad lips of the redeemed. Yet when we think about heaven, most of us find our memories journeying to a picture made up not of descriptions nor of details, but of what heaven is not. Once again the negative method of picturization has outlasted the extravagant affirmation of heaped-up superlatives. Heaven is the place where there is no darkness, no sea, no pain, no parting, no hunger, no death, no tears. So let us notice with confidence the things which Micah was not. For we may be able to make a respectable portrait from these negative colour-materials. The pigment may prove more satisfactory than we had supposed possible.

Micah is not autobiographical. Hosea spreads the story of his tortured heart for all " the daws to peck at." The happy dreams of his marriage days, the bitter realization of his doubts, the heart-breaking news of Gomer's cruel betrayal, the sobbing of his little brood, the long struggle while he fought his way back to manhood and confidence again, that drama-filled day when he saw her in her shame and loved her again, and bought her from her oppressors, and took her to his home,— these scenes are matchlessly vivid and frankly revealed. But Micah is secretive, hidden behind his sermons, utterly impersonal as far as his modest intentions control.

Micah is not a city man. Isaiah's life is touched at every point with the throbbing crowds of the metropolis. The pageantry of broad streets and mighty buildings, of vari-coloured processions, and sunlight and shadow, these things throng his mind. The sins he assails are city sins, the destiny he defends is a city destiny, the sympathy he feels is city sympathy, his heart is enthralled by the city. But Micah is the unsophisticated outlander, whose wits are sharp enough and whose eyes are keen enough to detect clearly the hollowness of city prides, and his language is the language of the hills, and his people are farm-people, embittered by the struggle with the stubborn poverty of agricultural slavery.

Micah is not a desert man. Amos came from barren Tekoa, where gaunt rocks and dreary wastes and straggling trees mocked the heroic effort of human beings to eke out an existence. His garments were shepherd's rags—the only trade he knew was the picayune business of pinching the sycamore buds to make them ripen into figs for selling. The sight of plenty drove him mad with frenzy and turned his wrath loose upon the pampered aristocrats who flaunted their wealth before his needs. But Micah came from the smiling acres of Moresheth, seventeen miles from Jerusalem, a rich land of well-tilled fields, and great strong trees, and plentiful harvests—where every prospect pleases, and only man is vile. Micah uttered no cry against prosperity as such. He did assail that brutal, futile selfishness which amasses senselessly, far beyond anyone's possible need, and vaunts itself in gestures of power over its neighbours.

Micah is not solitary. He does not burst alone upon a silent world. The voice of Amos has just died away upon the avenues of Bethel; Hosea has just sent his sob of pity down through Israel; Isaiah is still crying aloud those daring challenges to the king and the country, when Micah begins his preaching. He is no figure of lonely eminence.

Instead, he is a part of that mighty renaissance of prophecy which marked forever the eighth century before Christ.

Micah is not altogether unknown to us. Some of the favourite passages in the Bible came from his fertile mind. But, curiously enough, when we repeat these memorable sentences, we do not think of Micah as being responsible for them. His name has become unattached through the wear and tear of the centuries.

When we quote that beautiful prophecy, " But thou, Bethlehem-Ephrata, which art little to be among the thousands of Judah, out of thee shall come forth unto me one that is to be ruler in Israel; whose goings forth are of old, from everlasting. And he shall stand and shall feed his flock in the strength of Jehovah, in the majesty of the name of Jehovah his God; and they shall abide, for now he shall be great unto the ends of the earth," we ascribe those phrases not to Micah, but rather to Matthew, who reproduced them in his account of Jesus' birth.

When we read, " But in the latter days it shall come to pass that the mountain of Jehovah's house shall be established upon the top of the mountains, and it shall be exalted above the hills, and peoples shall flow unto it. And many nations shall go and

say, Come ye, and let us go up to the mountain of
Jehovah, and to the house of the God of Jacob;
and he will teach us of his ways and we will walk
in his paths. For out of Zion shall go forth the
law, and the word of Jehovah from Jerusalem, and
he will judge between many peoples, and will de-
cide concerning strong nations far off, and they
shall beat their swords into ploughshares and their
spears into pruninghooks; nation shall not lift up
sword against nation, neither shall they learn war
any more. But they shall sit every man under his
vine and fig-tree; and none shall make them
afraid; for the mouth of Jehovah, the Lord of
Hosts hath spoken it," we instinctively ascribe the
sentiment to Isaiah, refusing credit to Micah for
that growing dream of world-peace which has
become the most potent contribution of religion to
the modern mind.

When we memorize that all-inclusive statement
of the definition of religion, now a classic of sacred
expression, joining as it does the demand for social
serviceableness and individual personal purity of
spirit, " He hath showed thee, O man, what is
good; and what doth Jehovah require of thee but
to do justly, and to love kindness and to walk
humbly with thy God? ", we think of it as a dis-
tillation of the religious wisdom of the ages, rather

than as a daring venture by Micah into the formulation of faith. So it happens that while we repeat his truths often, and true our lives by his ideals constantly, he is lost behind his message, and his name is seldom spoken. He is one of our anonymous inspirers.

Micah is not a statesman. Isaiah dabbled eagerly in the political affairs of the realm. He brought the purpose of God to bear upon every plan of the king. He watched world events with keenest interest. He studied trends and analyzed national characters. He entered into every decision, counselling with all rulers, strengthening the people, fashioning as best he could the mould of the dynasties. But Micah has no word as to policies, cares not at all to advise about alliances, leaves the king to his own devices, and never thinks of God as devising specific directions for the ship of state.

Micah is not a ritualist. The Temple services may vary with the influence of this party or that. The words may change, the rites may meet new needs in new ways. But Micah goes his way, unconscious that God has any interest in the mere modes of formal religion, his mind on other things.

Micah is not a theologian. Hosea may boast as his outstanding contribution to the world his

picture of God as a loving redeemer. He may
spend his life carefully elaborating the implications
of that brilliant flash of theological truth. But
Micah has no new insight into the mind of God.
His preaching does not provide the illumination of
new concepts. We read his words in vain if we
expect creeds or formulations of philosophy in his
sermons.

Micah *was* the preacher who pitied the poor.
This is the one affirmation which we drag from
him. We have blocked off his profile in the sharp
silhouette of negation and contrast. There remains
the one revelation of his positive achievement. He
pitied the poor.

Even this we know not from his own boasting,
nor from the records of his neighbours' remembrance. We read it upon every page of his preaching, we see it in every gesture of his life; every
word he spoke was throbbing with the emotion of
his sympathy, every idea he had bore its pervad-
ing colour. He pitied the poor.

His mind was haunted with the remembered
sights of farmers, pitifully struggling with the re-
sisting soil of stubborn fields, succeeding at last in
their efforts to tame their meadows and cultivate
their farms only to have their whole achievement
stolen from them by the bold duplicity of rich

landlords, who foreclosed a mortgage and dispossessed the despondent tenants. His ears rang with the despair of debtors, caught in a hopeless tangle of obligations, their backs bent under the load of their fruitless labour, their souls harrowed with fear and want.

He revolted at the thought of respectable men, already rich beyond the dreams of avarice, spending their nights upon their beds plotting for fresh conquests, when they should have been quietly dreaming of better things. His ire rose when he recalled how pleasant, prosperous homesteads had been joined end to end in great estates, which plutocrats owned and managed, enslaving the toil of the poor. " They crop us as the sheep crop grass," he said. " They are cannibals, living upon the dripping snatches of writhing human flesh."

With this pitiful social contrast ever in his mind, we are confronted with the reason for his religious convictions. To a preacher like this, faith could never rest with being a correct form of prescribed worship. Why—he could remember that these powerful rich fiends in human form, but without the semblance of human kindness, clad in the garments of their ill-gotten gains, would all go to the Temple, and act through the forms of reverence day after day. It meant nothing to them, and they knew it. It meant nothing to the preacher who was forced to watch them. They were scoundrels even if the church did not dare label them. They were using their religion as a cloak for their greed.

To a prophet with such a background, religion could never seem to be merely a political philosophy for international relationships. These very same wealthy thieves were the leaders of influential national public opinion. They counseled with the king, they bargained with Assyria and Egypt for favourable alliances, they knew how certain was God's vengeance upon Israel's foes. Suppose Israel and Judah should by some freak of fate be forever guaranteed against foreign invasion, the poor people would still be helpless in the chains of these respectable brigands who rejoiced in the opportunities of absentee landlordism. The place to begin God's will was not off in the doubtful borderlands where foes menaced, but right here at home, upon these pleasant hillsides where waving grass and lowing cattle mocked the pitiful penury of the men who did the work.

To a man with a sympathy and an experience like that, religion could never be merely the subtlety of theological research. Interest in the task of finding out more things about God seemed of minor import before the terrible conviction that no one was paying any attention to the things already known about God. Why be so eager to explore the hidden corners of God's purposes, when here were hundreds of His explicit commands flagrantly disobeyed, and thousands of His pious people shamefully abused by fraud?

To Micah, religion meant inevitably and always a way of life—a quality of living and doing. Without that quality, correct forms were a mockery, pious politics a cowardly lie, and theological niceties were prim jokes upon reality.

How do you live? What do you do? Whom do you pity? Who has your sympathy? These were the simple, searching questions of his catechism.

Take the three favourite sayings of Micah which we have already quoted in full as representing his anonymous contribution to our literature and to our thinking. It is obvious that his outline of the definition of religion, his statement of the demands of the Lord upon His people, is couched in the frank unavoidable terms of personal piety and social sympathy. But the same is true of the other quoted paragraphs. His dream of pruninghooks and ploughshares is not a vaporous generalization in the direction of world peace. He sees even war in terms of the human beings whom it hurts and impoverishes and destroys. The climax of his prophecy of peace is reached when he envisions every man seated under his own vine and fig-tree, contented in the quiet happiness of personal owner-ship and personal independence. This, of course, is in direct contrast with the brutal contract system which in his own time made all tenants slaves, and all rich estate owners mammons of selfishness.

His distant glimpse at the coming Messiah, his naïve forecasting of the honour to Bethlehem, was but the focus of his hopes for justice—this king was to be a king of justice, before whom inhuman-ity should be destroyed, and in whose presence only brotherhood and shared joy could survive.

Of course, there is a certain definite concreteness in other forms of prophetic achievement which must prove tempting to a preacher. When we mix our religion in politics, we actually handle the measurable stuff of life, and our ideals may be enshrined in statutes. When we influence a change in the form of worship the addition persists in tangible form through centuries of ritual. And when we formulate a new conception of God, un-born generations of scholars will enter into the inheritance of our truth and call us blessed.

Compared with such assaults upon immortality, Micah seems to have chosen a way which was too easily erased. All he did was to present a certain sentiment which he thought pointed in the direction of a more everyday realistic religion. He wrote no laws, effected no alliances, dictated no rites,—he just embodied and encouraged a certain general religious pity, and he insisted that religion could not be recognized by him unless it pitied the poor.

But watch this unostentatious stream of influence broaden and deepen through the years. By the time Hezekiah's reign was drawing to its close, Isaiah was confessing that he could detect a fertile stream of warm religious sympathy blessing the whole life of Judah, and influencing every act of the capital. It began in the tiny trickling stream of Micah's brave pity. Deuteronomy records it flowing into laws of sympathy, of hospitality, of land ownership, of shared responsibility. Jesus brought it to its finest beauty in the great placid sea of kindness which was the central interest of his life. He went about doing good, he fed the hungry, healed the sick, helped the poor,—and when a wavering preacher sent from his prison a message to Christ, plaintively inquiring for any proofs that he was the authentic Saviour, Jesus replied, " Do you not see how I am helping people? The words of the prophet Micah, who pitied the poor, are being fulfilled in me."

Pity has not lost its charm today. Never did we need it more We have joined land to land. But we have also joined machine to machine, in vast batteries of factory sheds, and have drawn in workers from everywhere, from every country on the globe, to run our clattering automatons for us. Men do not own their own land today. They huddle in vast warrens of brick, thousands under one roof, waiting the owner's word that turns them out of these barracks and puts their children upon the streets. Men do not own their own tools of production today. Their jobs are at the mercy of a boss's whim. Masters lie upon soft couches at midnight, surrounded by every gift that limitless wealth can buy, plotting for more riches, though the treasure they now have hangs like a millstone around their necks.

Ledoux auctions men upon a slave-block in our public parks. Shop girls wear their young bodies into dreadful ugliness in the long hours of indefensible labour, and then face rich vice beckoning to them as they emerge in their exhaustion at night. Those who have the rule over them say their pious prayers at the correct times. They neglect nothing. The churches delight to honour them. They are correct and pleasant.

Oh, the pity of it! You say there is no cause

for pity? You insist that it is their own fault?
You draw up your garments and pass by? You
say that this is not religion?

You are twenty-five hundred years behind the
times. Never since Micah spoke have men dared
to say that religion was not pity, and pity not
religion.

V

THE PREACHER WHO LOVED THE
WORD—ZEPHANIAH

READ Zephaniah as a book, and you will turn away convinced that it is only another echo of the oft-repeated prophetic doom. The same deep lamentation, the same blame for pagan foes, the same justification of God's wrath, the same despair for an unrepentant Israel—here is nothing but a restatement of the sad fate of the chosen people, with a lingering glint of hope for them if they will seek the Lord again. Three pages are sufficient to contain his message in the text of our English Bibles, and the pages seem almost wasted upon the monotony of vain repetition.

View Zephaniah as a figure in history, and you will turn away convinced that he was almost a nonentity. His traces survive between the narrow boundaries of this brief book. His name appears here only. He is not mentioned in the accounts of the kingdom's vicissitudes. His voice rises for a moment above the babble of the world's many tongues, and then is lost in silence.

But view him as a human preacher, labouring for his faith against a background of human environment, and he becomes the acme of romance. Watch him as he guards his dream, plans his campaign, battles with terrible difficulties, and at last wins through to a glorious victory. This prophet's story was an adventure with breathless incidents and a classic climax.

His name means "Hidden by God." At once we are plunged into the midst of the terrible days of Manasseh, when the boy Zephaniah was born. His ancestors' names, reaching back through four generations of goodly heritage, bring us at last to Hezekiah, that godly king whom all good men honoured, and from whose line Zephaniah sprang. Yet when this boy was born, in the blessed piety of a faith-filled home, so wildly irreligious was the ruling monarch, so cruel his lust for the blood of all who carried on the tradition of reverence, so outspoken his program of bestial killing, that the boy's parents decided to conceal this newcomer, hoping for better days when persecution would be no more, and it would be safe to bring up a boy in the nurture and admonition of the Lord. When they named him, they called him Zephaniah, "Hidden of God."

Living in such a home, the tradition of the blessed word must have been his from the outset. He knew the holy phrases of God's law, he loved the vivid stories of God's dealings with His people, his voice joined often in the heartening songs of Zion. He was fed upon the nourishment of faith. As a boy, the seal of God's call was upon him and his life was consecrated to the guarding of God's truth.

But around this pious household, the tumult of heathen raging rose like an angry sea. Manasseh, whose fiery threats introduced the "killing days" which were to go down through history like a bad dream, added insult to injury by setting up shrines of worship in honour of brutal Assyrian deities, and by urging his people to reverence the hosts of heaven whose names he had learned from his vile neighbours. Amon, who followed him on the throne, bore a name which witnessed to his dedication for the service of pagan faiths, and he did not choose to belie his name. Within a few brief months, he was slaughtered by jealous and resentful palace-servants, who seized his power for themselves, and set themselves up as rulers. These same servant-monarchs saw their ambitions totter when loyalists attacked them and placed upon the throne a little boy of royal blood, not old enough to know his own mind—that wistful lad, Josiah.

While this lurid drama was being enacted within the palace gates, the nation was sinking back into sullen indifference. Zephaniah was doing his best to keep the truth of God hidden and unharmed, but the people were lost, like sheep who wandered without a reasonable shepherd. Their minds and hearts could not be adjusted to the sudden shifts in official religion which the ill-fated dynasties in turn prescribed. So they weakly conformed to the ritual demands, while religion meant less and less of reality to them. The first message of Zephaniah reveals the state of their aloofness to all spiritual and social and moral claims.

" I will search Jerusalem with lights," warns the God who speaks through Zephaniah. " I will not spare the people who are caught in the vice of indifference. My people are settled back upon their lees, like vile, stale tea, all freshness gone—the only flavour left being the dead bitterness of sloth."

These people say in their heart, " Jehovah will not do good, neither will he do evil." The depths of sophisticated callousness had been reached. God had become a mere abstraction. No one expected him to do anything. Courage would go unnoticed and unrewarded. Cowardice would escape attention and punishment. No one need worry nor try. The tang had gone out of life. No one cared any more.

There can be imagined no more difficult congregation for the preacher. Zephaniah was forced to lash out against a city that lived carelessly and thoughtlessly. Long ago it was discovered that God's causes are very seldom defeated by the hot assaults of the devil. Instead, the divine purposes suffer from the slow, crushing glacier-like mass of ten thousand times ten thousand nobodies who are unimportant in themselves and who do not care what happens. God's plans are not blasted into destruction. They are sat upon by the dead weight of cool unconcerned people who are not particularly *against*, but who are certainly not particularly *for*.

It was this deadening sin which Jesus was later so fiercely to despise. You are either for me or against me, he boldly announced. It was the lukewarm church which was spewed from the mouth of the conquering monarch, Christ, in that devastating picture of the last days. A cold church might have been rebuked, and a hot church might have been used, but a lukewarm church—bah!— nothing can be done with it. Nor with a lukewarm

man. Nor with a lukewarm nation, such as this
nation which surrounded Zephaniah.

The greatest cowards in the world are not the
people who in sudden panic run away. The greatest cowards are the people who blandly say, " Go
ahead, I am willing." And when they say " willing," they mean that they will interpose no particular objection if you go ahead. You need count
upon no active opposition from them. Into what
low estate has that fine word " willing " been
dragged. There was a day when to say " I am
willing " meant " I am will-ing," " I am for it with
all my will," " I am bending my will to accom-
plish it." Now it means, " I am indifferent enough
so that you need not fight me in order to do it."
How have the mighty words fallen!

Now, the Jerusalem which surrounded Zephaniah
was not " will-ing " anything. It was just indif-
ferently " willing." And often Zephaniah must
have longed for a taste of good, old-fashioned bitter
opposition, in place of the dreadful clamminess of
tolerant softness. At least this would have told
him what he was saying was reaching some hearts
and minds. Even this doubtful blessing was
denied him. For a modern picture of the cruelty
of indifference, we need only turn to G. Studdert-
Kennedy's striking poem:

> " *When Jesus came to Golgotha, they hanged him
>   to a tree,*
> *They drave great nails through hands and feet,
>   they made a Calvary.*
> *They crowned him with a crown of thorns, red
>   were his wounds and deep,*
> *For those were crude and cruel days, and
>   human flesh was cheap.*

> " *When Jesus came to Birmingham, they only
>   passed him by,*
> *They did not hurt a hair of him, they only let
>   him die,*
> *For men had grown more tender and they would
>   not give him pain,*
> *They only passed him in the street and left him
>   in the rain.*

> " *Still Jesus prayed, 'Forgive them, for they
>   know not what they do,'*
> *And still it rained the winter rain that drenched
>   him through and through.*
> *The crowds went home and left the streets with
>   no one there to see,*
> *And Jesus crouched against the wall and cried
>   for Calvary."*

We are killing Christ today, not by cruel nails
and sharp thorns; we simply pass him by. No
wonder that he cries for Calvary. Death by indifference is the cruelest fate.

In the midst of this careless throng, Zephaniah
did his best to be a true prophet. However little
they cared, he loved the sacred word with all his
heart. However lightly they listened, he strained

to catch the first faint accents of Jehovah's voice. However vilely they sinned, he kept his life pure and clean, ready for consecrated service. " O, how love I Thy law. It is my meditation, day and night. It is a lamp to my feet, that I might not sin against Thee. How long, O Lord, how long— ere I can pass these blessed laws of Thine on to someone who will heed and love? "

Then, as suddenly as a lightning flash, his chance came. The little boy-king, whom nobody knew and of whom nobody could be sure, began to ask about the things of faith. The bed-rock of manly character began to show through the pleasant beauty of his youth. He broke with the traditions of those bloody kings who preceded him, he disdained the blandishments of sin and the lying lures of selfish power, and by that miracle of grace which sometimes rescues a people when they do not deserve rescue, God made of Josiah a good man determined to be a good king. " He was eight years old when he began to reign. And he did that which was right in the sight of the Lord. He walked in the way of David his father, and turned not aside to the right hand or the left."

What a thrill swept over the anxious soul of Zephaniah. He had prayed through the darkness of despair. He had hoped against hope. He had preached holiness in the midst of defilement. He had spoken for Jehovah when all men were reviling Him. He had kept the Holy Word while all the world was scoffing. Now he was to see the fruition of all his dreams.

The lad yielded to the influence of faith while Zephaniah waited with bated breath. How large a part this prophet had in the royal schooling, we cannot tell. Perhaps he often spoke with the tiny monarch about his hopes in the Lord. Perhaps he only stood afar off, hoping and praying and rejoicing. His name never emerges out of the records of the time. Other courtiers are listed, but not he. The high priest is cited, prophets and priests, prophetesses, and scribes are named, but not Zephaniah. Yet through it all, he was remembering that when those honored names were all unknown, he was stolidly helping to keep the Book of God's law safe from the frenzy of a mad, faithless nation. And in all his denunciation of the frightful life that swirled like a whirlpool round him, there is no single word of criticism for Josiah. Zephaniah the prophet was not censoring him. He was praying for him. And the longing of his heart yearned that the boy might prove true to the sacred wisdom which he was learning.

The great day has arrived. A priest finds the

Book of the Law in the House of the Lord. The
words are borne to Josiah. The king reads through
the solemn demands for holiness which Jehovah
prescribes for His people. A sense of shame fills
the king's heart as he sees how far short he has
come, and how grievously his people have sinned.
He rends his clothes in repentance. Then the
full significance of these mighty commandments
reaches his chastened heart. He knows that he
has found a law, not for himself alone, but for
his people.

The trumpets blow. The elders of Judah as-
semble. The people of Jerusalem throng the temple gates. Before them stands the young king
with the scroll of the Law before him. He lifts
his voice and reads those resounding syllables
which the decades of wickedness had concealed and
almost destroyed. People and priests, young and
old, listen and understand. Then before them all,
the monarch announces a new covenant, between
himself and his people and his God. "We shall
walk after the Lord and keep his commandments
and his testimonies and his statutes with all our
hearts, and with all our soul, to perform the
words of the covenant which are written in this
book."

Then he causes all who are present in Jerusalem

to stand to it. And the inhabitants of Jerusalem stand and swear, and then depart to do, according to the covenant of their God, the God of their fathers.

It was a happy king who left the Temple that day, his mind glad for the favour of a guiding God who doeth all things well. They were happy people who hurried home that day, conscience-clear, soul-cleansed, with the redeeming glory of a great religious revival experience. But happiest of all was a single, unhonoured preacher. He had mingled with the crowd. He had heard the trumpets sounding. He had seen the young king. He had listened to the reading.

He had not been asked to take a place with the priests in the seats of honour. People who saw him had not realized what share he was having in the proceedings. No one could suspect the secret joy which flowed like a quiet river through his heart.

But his soul was exulting and his eyes were gleaming with tears of happiness. His name was Zephaniah. This was his day. These were his dreams come true. This was the Book of the Law that he had helped to preserve. This was the little king whose life he had surrounded with his anguished prayers. This was his hour of triumph.

His guardianship was at an end. The years of waiting were over. God had given him this great day of victory. Now he was ready to die.

Did he care because others surrounded the king and beamed down upon the happy multitude? Did he resent hearing other names—Hilkiah, the high priest; Shachan, the scribe; Huldah, the prophetess,—mentioned in the exultant chatter of the throng? Did he covet some of the public honour for himself? Nay, he had his rich reward. The happiest man in Jerusalem that day was Zephaniah, the preacher who had helped to keep the Word of the Lord intact through the night of doubt and sin, and who now saw that very Word which he had loved beginning to rule his nation's life.

Across the centuries, he preaches to us—this prophet who loved and honoured and defended the Sacred Book. We need the message of Isaiah, to keep us fighting when compromise allures. Amos must show us the shamefulness of our aristocratic prides. Hosea must sob out God's love for us. Micah must weep with us over the pangs of the pitiful poor.

But with all these, we need the rebuke of Zephaniah, who rails at our indifference and bids us passionately love our Book. Tyndale loved it enough to die that we might read it without fear or error.

Englishmen have traded loads of hay for a few minutes with one of its pages. Alice Collins learned two chapters of it when a little girl, and went all over Britain, reciting the precious words to delighted Christians. An Indian chief taught his stubborn seventy-year-old brain to master English, simply that he might hear his own Bible speak again and again to him, and he counted the years of desperate study a price all too small for the precious privilege which it brought him.

We, who buy millions of Bibles every year—we, who can buy a complete edition for a shilling— we read the muck of daily journalism while the Bible gathers dust upon our shelves.

I heard Russell Conwell speak to a vast throng of boys and girls, in Philadelphia, just before his death. The solemn sense of a valedictory was upon the crowd that night. It had touched his own heart and made every word rich with meaning. He pleaded with them to love and read their Bible. If he could have followed us out of his church that night—if he could have seen a thousand youngsters bending over the sacred pages of the Holy Book, reading with tear-dimmed eyes before sleep came that night—he would have felt that same uplifting joy which crowned Zephaniah's ministry, when Josiah pledged the nation to God's law.

If a preacher does not love the Word, what right
has he to preach from it?   If criticism and textual
analysis have spoiled the Book for him, let him
frankly confess it and cease from the mounte-
bankery of pretense.   If seminaries confuse minds
with smatterings of the original Hebrew and Greek,
and offer no comprehensive acquaintance with the
whole English Bible, let them take the consequences and stand forever convicted of their
failure.

But if you love the Word—then really love it,
and read it and defend it, and live it!   Some day,
on the edge of the rejoicing crowd of humanity,
your own heart will kindle with a joy that few can
know.   Some day, mankind will yield to the Word.
Then your prayers will have their answer.   Into
the joy of Zephaniah you will be admitted, blood-
brother of his unflagging faithfulness and of his
indescribable happiness.

VI

THE PREACHER WHO LAUGHED AT
FOES—NAHUM

CONSIDER the situation. For years, Israel and Judah had been paying tribute-money to satisfy the rapacious hunger of pagan imperialism. The armies of Babylon and Nineveh had swept back and forth in the ecstasy of conquering and the despair of defeat. Assyria and Egypt had threatened each other across the helpless stretch of intervening country, and had made of Galilee a bloody Belgium.

All around, great cities were rising into proud power and falling again into pitiable ruin. Babylon reared her confident head, Nineveh drew her hordes of citizens, Thebes began collecting an army of world-threatening dimensions. Meanwhile, Jerusalem, the favoured city of Jehovah, bearing upon her fate the promise of surpassing glory, remained by contrast an unimportant settlement, without adequate defenses—her king a puppet in the hands of that empire whose star was for

the moment in the ascendancy. There was no vast
wave of growth to brighten her hopes for world
conquest, no hero arose to hurl new assaults upon
her ancient foes, she had become a toy with which
boasting monarchs played for a moment, while
they dallied between conflicts. If hope deferred
maketh the heart sick, the faithful in Jerusalem
were being tested with the tragic tortures of continued disappointment.

For a brief moment, there was a flash of promise
on the horizon. Thebes rose in sudden might to
threaten a disturbance in that dreadful balance of
power which had made Israel and Judah into
shambles. Praying hearts trembled with the anticipation that perhaps Thebes was to be the
answer to their prayers. All hope of mercy from
Assyria, from Egypt, from Babylon, from Nineveh,
had vanished. If they continued to wax great,
Jerusalem's fate was sealed in gloom. But with
that optimism which rises only out of black despair,
there were those who hoped that Thebes might
crush all the existing empires, and in her victory
might be merciful to God's chosen people.

Then Thebes collapsed, in a vast cataclysm of
destruction. The roar of her ruin silenced the pitiable petitions of Israel. The dust of her defeat
blinded the eyes of Judah and they saw no longer

the dream of God's promise. Now the deepest blackness of their night of woe had been reached. They were, of all people, most miserable. They could sing no more. They could trust no more. They could pray no more. Their faith had turned to dust and ashes upon their lips. Their God had deserted them after fair words and lying promises. Had he ever existed, this shattered Jehovah of theirs? Was there ever any truth in him? How could he survive the continued defiance of Gog and Magog, of Osiris, of Bel and the Bull-God of Nineveh?

The dull murmur of hopeless despair from the lips of the old mingled with harsh clamour of young voices—sure that Jehovah had never been anything more real than a mocking dream, that the prophets have been servants of a blatant lie, and that the bright city of the New Jerusalem was a phantasy which flickered like a mirage to tempt the tired souls of God's people across the burning deserts of history. "Of course, the mirage has vanished now, and we shall never again allow our-selves to be deceived." Thus spoke the saddened voices of the men of Jerusalem.

Suddenly, out of the murmur and clamour, comes a great outburst of laughter. It rings down the sad avenues of God's city. It echoes out over the hills of Judah. It sounds like a trumpet-call over the valleys of Israel. Laughter—laughter—laughter— while people stand aghast!

Is this man mad? Is this the futile glee of a maniac? Does he know the situation? Has he been blind to the tokens of despair?

Or is he feigning? Is this a startling device to freeze our souls into immediate attention?

He is sane, this laughing preacher. He has seen everything there is to be seen—he knows all about the blackness of the circumstances—he needs no coaching in the facts of defeat. And he is utterly sincere, laughingly confident of the indomitable, invincible power of God. Under the roar of his laughter we can catch the syllables, " The Lord— the Lord—shall hold them in derision! He will laugh aloud at them! "

This is Nahum's contribution to the literature of prophecy. Isaiah had said, " God wants you to keep on fighting." Amos had insisted, " God can use any one of you." Micah had comforted, " God forgives you even when you fail." Zephaniah had thundered, " God will tolerate no lukewarm indifference."

But Nahum lifted his voice in the night of his people's despair, and shouted to the silent skies, " God cannot be beaten! " All this seeming triumph on the part of His foes is but illusion. Nineveh is doomed. All who neglect Jehovah will be beaten back. There is no defeat for Jerusalem. Opposition is folly. Armies and chariots are chaff before His wind. The universe fights for God. He cannot be beaten! Doubt is folly. Laugh at them—laugh at them—laugh at them! The Lord will roar with laughter!

This blood-curdling, heart-clutching flood of derision shocks us like a shriek.

It is the only thing we know about Nahum which makes him rise in distinction from his fellows. His name means " Consolation," but its meaning must have seemed singularly inappropriate, for if there was one note he refused to sound, it was the note of consolation. " Consolation? There is nothing to console about, and no one who needs consolation! God is winning; His foes are in His hands; and only fools refuse to believe it! " Had his parents foreseen his life, they would not have thought of him as " consolation."

He was born in El-kosh, but El-kosh itself is a puzzle, and the name means only a cause for dispute among antiquarians and archæologists. His family, his training, his fate, are all hidden from us. There is a casket still preserved where one may see what guides will claim to be his bones.

But this is only another tradition made of the mists of fancy and romance.

We sense in the rounded sentences of his message the skill of a great poet. Language was beauty to him, words were lovely threads to be skilfully used in the fabric of thought. He knew the ecstasy of effective speech.

But this is the only trace of him which survives. He proposed no single suggestion for Israel's reform. He had no comment on the social conditions which surrounded him. His heart offered no forgiveness to those who flaunted their pride before Jehovah. He had no brooding offer of mercy to the faithless, no revelation of the nature of God's mind. Down through the centuries come the strident syllables of his laughter—he is content. God cannot be beaten!

Listen to its echoes, as the tale of history unfolds:

Judas Maccabæus hears it, when Syria has risen to imperial supremacy and the Seleucidæ are treading out the life of the world. His own heart responds. He counts his life as nothing. He cuts loose from all encumbrances. He refuses to count his foes and his own forces. He will have nothing to do with reasonable military computations. He is not interested in the cautious injunctions of his

friends bidding him be sane and yield, at least for
the time, to the terrible threats of Syria's might.
He knows only that God cannot be beaten. He
speaks no syllable. He laughs. The line of Jewish
courage stiffens into bright heroism. The laughter
spreads from home to home. The Syrians hear it,
over the walls, as they wait for the moment to seize
their prey. And the faith of Israel, flickering like a
dying flame and about to vanish in a thin wisp of
gray smoke, blazes up again, burns in a fury of
protest for years, and then settles down into steady
beauty. God cannot be beaten!

Jesus hears it. The shadow of the Cross is upon
him. The foes are thronging outside. His little
band of disciples are huddled together like frightened sheep before the threat of the swirling storm.
The world has not yet heard of him. The darkness of sin and hate is engulfing all that he said
and did. Then he laughs and says, " I have over-
come the world! " God cannot be beaten!

The Coliseum hears it. Wild beasts are howling
in their cages. A huge throng massed on the serried
benches yells for blood. An emperor sits upon
silken and velvet cushions, his women around him,
his sycophants near him. The signal is given. The
barred gates are open. The lions leap forward.
Silence grips the crowd. There in the centre a

little knot of people are kneeling in silent prayer. They stand to their feet. Upon their faces is no fear. Their eyes gleam with courage. They begin to sing, the simply harmony of some Christian hymn. And as the fangs of cruel beasts invade their flesh, as sharpened talons rip their limbs apart, these men and women laugh! God cannot be beaten!

Luther hears it, as he mounts the church steps and nails upon the door the pronouncement of his determination. The schools will scorn him, his friends will sneer at him, his church will persecute him—but " Here I stand! I can do no other! God help me! " And a peal of defiant laughter sounds through the words. God cannot be beaten!

Tyndale hears it, while the flames mount up to consume his broken, writhing body. They have destroyed his English-printed New Testament; they have cursed him as if he were a moral leper spreading the contagion of his sins through innocent homes; they have exiled him, and starved him, and libelled him, and fought him with maniacal fury in the name of Jesus. Now at last they have caught him in a trap of deceit, and have led him off to die. The leaves of his books perish so easily, words are forgotten so soon, this old body will in

a few moments be a charred ember of irrecogniz-
able flesh. But he laughs through the blaze, and
his lips say confidently, " God, open the king of
England's eyes! " God cannot be beaten!

Pitken hears it, as the Boxer fiends climb over
the wall of his Chinese mission compound and
brandish their knives in glee. He uses his last
moments to say a word to his native servant,
" Take word to my wife," he says. " Tell her to
send our boy to some good school until he is ready
to preach. And tell her, then, to send him back
here to China where they killed me! " Then he
turned and laughed, while the blades hacked him
into ribbons of flesh. God cannot be beaten!

Were they mad, these men? Had Nahum
started an epidemic of futile insanity? If this be
madness, God give us more of their madness today.
" A coward will call himself a wary man," said
Bacon. God keep us from being so wary that we
are not brave. We have enough of that cool
scientific accuracy which balances statistics against
statistics, and gives meticulous estimates of chances
for victory. God give us some of that frenzied
madness which overrides all forecasting, and
knows that God cannot be beaten. We have
enough of that pitiable human breed which sees
the difficulty in every opportunity. We could

stand a few more heroes like Nahum, who will see the opportunity in every difficulty.

One day my great gray cruiser, the North Carolina, was nursing a convoy of troop-ships through the submarine zones of the North Atlantic. We saw the sudden flashes of gun-fire, and heard the barking defiance of three-inch shells—watched the geysers leap up to mark the detonation of death-bombs—and dimly descried the tracks of a periscope where a U-boat was skulking. At once the thrilling bugle-call " Battle-stations! " was sounded, and we scurried to our places.

My own duty took me down into the bowels of the ship, to direct a hospital dressing-station equipped for surgical care of the wounded. Crowded into the steel compartment, near the engine room, far below the water-line, we waited and tried to look brave.

The little guns were chattering up on the deck, the turrets were booming and thundering, the engines were throbbing with furious effort, telephone bells were jangling here and there. Now and then the whole ship would heave in a monstrous convulsion, and rock back and forth in a shiver of apprehension, as a mammoth depth-bomb, intended for the submarine, cut loose in our vicinity. And we would think, " This is exactly how a torpedo would sound, if it hit us. But we would never know the difference! "

Suddenly, down through the passage-ways, we heard a rollicking wave of laughter. From corridor to corridor it passed. Men were shouting in glee and slapping each other on the back as they repeated the hilarious news. "Hey! What do you know about that? Peterson threw his shoe at the submarine! He was up on the quarter-deck, when she shot her periscope up, right under his nose, and began to look around. He watched her for just a moment, and then he laughed and slipped off his shoe and threw it at the U-boat. What do you know about that? "

All fear had gone. All anxiety had disappeared. We could do anything now? Peterson had thrown his shoe—Ha, ha, ha!

Come, Christians, let us send a wave of laughter echoing through the Church. We are so tense, so solemn, so serious, so sober, so statistical. Lawlessness frightens us. Indifference discourages us. Quarrels weaken us. Foes assail us and we withdraw. We are in doubt as to our power. We question if we can ever win. Has God forsaken us?

Laugh—laugh with us! God cannot be beaten!

Laugh while our enemies quail. Laugh while we start forward. Laugh at their swollen pride. Echo the defiance of Nahum. Pick up the syllables from the lips of Jesus. The Lord will have them in derision. God cannot be beaten!

VII

THE PREACHER WHO DOUBTED GOD—
HABAKKUK

HIS name was Habakkuk. In those days names meant something. They were not carelessly appended out of the confusion of the first few days of life. Names were intended to indicate something of interest and enlightenment about the person named.

This boy's name meant " Embrace," " The Little One Who Embraced," " The Little Clinging Boy." I think I can see him now as I repeat his name. For I have known just such little boys and have loved them. He was one of those affectionate, sensitive, wistful lads; his lips would tremble so easily; his big eyes would start into tears at a moment's notice. He could enjoy things to the very limit when they were all beautiful and bright. He could bubble over with a happy glorious glee. But oh, how he could suffer when something disappointed him! How his little heart broke when a cherished plan was shattered! How he retreated within himself when someone he loved betrayed a trust!

He was a musician, trained to play upon stringed instruments. No one can revel in the delights of harmony like a musician. There is an ecstasy about an exquisite chord which no mere layman can approach. It is the trained performer who understands artistic enjoyment at its best. But oh, how terribly discord pains a true musician! Blunderers and amateurs might hear a piano out of tune and never know the difference. A slight shift off key would hardly spoil a day for most of us. But for one whose ear is trained to detect the slightest variation in pitch, there can be no torture quite like the jangling notes of an imperfect instrument, or the blurred outline of a poorly executed arpeggio. Disharmony is unimaginably poignant to one who knows the finest possibilities of chords and progressions.

It was because he was that kind of a boy, and because he was that kind of a musician, that Habakkuk became the kind of a prophet he was. He was the preacher who doubted God.

He carried over into his manhood that wistful sensitiveness to disappointment, and the cruel facts of life broke his heart. Disharmony, whenever he detected it, racked him with its pain, and when he heard the jangling chords of human misery and jealousy and hate, he could not stand the strain of the experience.

Josiah had just died after a reign which began with glorious promise and ended with a fine show of substantial reform. But the seeds of sin had been sown deep in the soil of the nation, and they were only waiting for a favourable opportunity to break forth in a riot of choking stubborn weeds.

Jehoiachim ascended the throne. A few brief days were enough to reveal that his path would lead away from Josiah's purposes. Cruel, lustful, fiendish, and selfish, he stamped his nation with the superscription of his own nature, and proved how quickly destruction can overwhelm the finest of human foundations. One swift slash of a knife could ruin the Mona Lisa. One week of Jehoiachim had wrecked the structure of Josiah's striving.

From the monarch, the people took their own mood. Lawlessness broke out like a conflagration. The steady habits of the years gave way to the wanton abuses of sudden license. The book of the law was spurned while men spat upon it. The priests were scorned. Religion was conveniently shelved where it could interpose no interference in the vast orgies of daily life.

Outside the borders of the land, great waves of scornful opposition were rising. First Assyria, then Egypt, then Chaldea, trampled upon the tiny buffer-state, in a succession of brutal conquerings, reaching a bloody climax in Habakkuk's day. The disdain with which these brutal hosts clattered through God's Chosen Land, the utter wantonness with which they devoured what they desired, and destroyed what they did not care to devour, the hideous cruelty which cared not at all for human life when it seemed to be interposed before the advance of a cherished imperial dream,—these things saddened the heart of Jerusalem. What they did for the sensitive spirit of the prophet Habakkuk can be but faintly imagined. Life looked to him like a cruel chase, in which the fowlers flung their nets again and again over the helpless flocks of these frightened people, to capture and torment and destroy them in the grim glee of sport.

It is for this reason that Habakkuk spoke not for God to the people, but for the people to God. All the other prophets were proud to bear a message from Jehovah as His representative to the waiting hosts. Isaiah had proclaimed upon the authority of God that the proposed compromises with heathen powers were examples of treacherous cowardice. Amos held the sins of his sophisticated generation up to feel the scorn of a righteous Ruler. Micah exposed the pity in the heart of God as He looked upon the wretched poor, and stung the indifferent rich into sympathy. Hosea revealed the infinite merciful desire to forgive and forgive and forgive again. Zephaniah spent his life in protecting and defending and proclaiming a message from God which the people were not disposed to hear. Nahum sent a thrilling wave of laughter from the throne of God to stiffen the resistance of his wavering people. But it remained for Habakkuk to begin a prophetic career by voicing a protest, not from an outraged God to a guilty people, but from an outraged people to an offending, neglecting, indifferent God. He was advocate, not of God, but of his nation.

The very word prophet means one who speaks on God's behalf—the mouthpiece of the Divine will—God's representative among men. In this sense, Habakkuk hardly deserved the name. For his words were addressed to God—the cause he was pleading was the cause of his bewildered countrymen.

Out from his pain-racked life came the cry, "How long, O Lord, how long? We are like worms before thee." All the woeful sensitiveness of his boy-heart, all the tortured agony of his musician's soul, voiced themselves in his poignant plea, as he lifted his broken people up before God's eyes for pity, and prayed for their relief. And his suffering reached its depths in that bitter blasphemy of doubt, "When we call, you do not hear!"

Suppose that he had suppressed his complaints in silence. He must have been tempted to do so. For we are trained by our religious exercises to be slightly ashamed of our questionings. We are proud of our ability to take things for granted in our faith. We are embarrassed by the sense that our queries are really secret disloyalties masking themselves as innocent questions, and should be discouraged.

Young people see this trait in the Church today, and they distrust us because we affect to blush when someone dares to utter a doubt. We try to hush our questions under a show of embarrassment. But this doubting preacher refused to yield to the temptation of loyal silence. He would not conform supinely to the correct creed of doctrinal affirmation. He wanted to know how and why. He realized that the only way to find out was to throttle his ceremonial politeness for the time being and frankly phrase his scepticism. So the words rose from his tortured lips, and bursting in a wave of indignant complaint and protest he cried out, "How long, O Lord, how long? We are like worms before thee. When we call, you do not hear!"

He expected that God, if there was a God, would rebuke him for his doubts. He thought of Jehovah as drawing aside from these queries in offended majesty, as if the questions were brazen insults full of disloyalty. Instead, God welcomed the chance to answer the questions, for this man and then for all the doubting world. Habakkuk's fears were routed. This did he gain by candid asking. But the fears of mankind were dispelled in the same transaction, so long as mankind has the wit to read the solutions which God here proposed.

Every doubt frankly expressed opens the way for an answer to that particular doubt if an answer exists. But it also opens the way for an answer to all such doubts which haunt the puzzled minds of men. Every doubt shamefacedly repressed makes it harder for other doubters to find the solution which they seek. "Prove me, now, saith the Lord." He does not fear questions. It is not a tribute to Him to protect Him from doubts. There is more faith in honest doubts than all your pious creeds.

Up to the top of a solitary high tower God led Habakkuk. Away from the clamour of the crowd, away from the dust of the battle, far enough above for a long view of things—this tear-stained preacher climbed. Have you a high tower somewhere in your life? You need tell no one else where it is. Habakkuk never revealed the location of his place of Divine trysting. But every life needs to find a spot where God waits in the silence to reveal eternity's secrets about the baffling scene called life. I pity most those forlorn souls who, plunged into the heat of the desperate fray, have no chance to escape for a time, and at a distance, " view the landscape o'er," for their soul's good.

There, above the tumult of life, God gave this questioning, baffled preacher two lessons for his courage and his patience. It was a solitary place and God met with him alone, but after the lessons had been revealed, God counseled him to refuse to keep them to himself, but to pass them on for all mankind to share. " Write the vision, so that it might last through all generations. Write it so that all who run may read. Others have suffered and have not found the secret of the high tower. Others will suffer and will need the strength I have given you. They may be disheartened unless you tell them my truth." So the preacher who doubted and dared to say his doubts in the very face of God, became a prophet in deed, proclaiming from God a reply which had satisfied him and which was intended to satisfy us.

Has it really lasted through the centuries in its freshness and encouragement? We are so often tempted to run. Is it written large enough so that we who run may read, and thus take courage again? Traces of that suffering which drove Habakkuk to the high tower, are upon our lives as we flee from the awful implications of the world's mocking cruelties. O let us have the truth the doubting preacher discovered!

This is the first revelation, out of the heart of God. The wicked will fail. Glance down the annals of history. The wicked always fail. Chaldea seems to be raised up in pride and conquering glory now. But Chaldea is not invulnerable. Chaldea will yield to the will of God. Every foe wears himself out in the vain repetition of futile assaults. This seeming prosperity of the wicked which discourages you is only illusion. They are all puffed up and swollen with their boastings. The more startling will be their collapse when the day of the Lord comes upon them. The hammers do not hurt the anvil. Do not waste your sympathy. Their blows seem cruel and hard to bear. But watch through the years and you will discover that it is the hammer which wears out, while the anvil survives.

All this may not appear upon the surface of the experience in which you dwell. The crises may seem tragic in their significance at the point in the conflict where you are engaged. But one look at the map of the whole line, seen as a whole, will convince you that only victory is possible. Let the high tower lift you above yourself. Glance at the contour of the continent on which the foes are battling. See the steadily advancing line of God's truth. Then back to the fight with a heart for any sacrifice. God will bring the victory. Be confident in Him.

But even confidence is not enough. The most assured courage sometimes seems most grievously disappointed. You know you can trust God. Once you are sure of that, be patient. God's victories take time. You little human individuals are so restive.

> "A toadstool grows up in a night,
>   Learn the lesson, little folk,—
> An oak grows on a hundred years,
>   But then, it is an oak."

Other things may seem for the time more impressive. Thunder and tempests may frighten and dismay, but at the last, God is in the still, small voice. The Lord is in His holy temple—the righteous shall live by His faithfulness.

> "The mills of the gods grind slowly, but they
> grind exceeding small."

Broken-hearted, shattered, tortured prophet,— you are clinging desperately like a frightened boy. You are holding God in your bewildered embrace. Keep hold. Cling to Him. Some day you will see that your faith is truth and your doubts are lies.

> "Truth forever on the scaffold, wrong forever
> on the throne.—
> Yet that scaffold sways the future, and behind
> the dim unknown,
> Standeth God within the shadow, keeping watch
> above His own."

It is this ability to see through the apparent disasters of circumstance, into the real triumph of eternity, which constitutes the essence of faith. Faith is the substance of things hoped for, the evidence of things not seen.

"Wherefore we faint not, but though our outward man is decaying, yet our inward man is renewed day by day. For this light affliction, which is for the moment, worketh for us more and more exceedingly an eternal weight of glory, while we look, not at the things which are seen, but at the things which are not seen, for the things which are seen are temporal, but the things which are not seen are eternal."

And to be able to carry this confidence down from the tower of faith into the stress of the fighting—to sacrifice more fully and more freely because we know that we cannot lose—this is the genius of the Christian life.

" Therefore let us also, seeing we are compassed about with so great a cloud of witnesses, lay aside every weight and the sin which doth so easily beset us, and let us run with patience the race that is set before us, looking unto Jesus, the author and perfecter of our faith, who for the joy that was set before him, endured the cross, despising shame, and hath sat down at the right hand of the throne of God. For consider him that hath endured such contradiction of sinners against himself, that ye wax not weary, fainting in your souls."

Let this faith be in us, which was also in Christ Jesus our Lord. And in ancient Habakkuk, surrounded by a sea of troubles.

VIII

THE PREACHER WHO BURIED HIS CLOTHES—JEREMIAH

HERE, at last, is a preacher whose life is crystallized in a sizable treasure of literature. And we claim the right to voice our relief.

For, with some of these ancient messengers, the task of reconstructing their lives has been unquestionably difficult. They tell us that there are biological experts who can take a single prehistoric fossil-bone, and, with this as the sole clue, can build up the corresponding skeleton, clothe it with the appropriate hide, and present to the wondering layman's eyes the facsimile of the animal whose only trace was one fragment. But the process always seems dubious, and is certainly fraught with much danger of error. Yet something of the kind has been necessary in order to realize the personalities of these prophets whose lives were almost completely obliterated by the passage of time. Only a name, plus a verse or two of narrative, plus a paragraph of preaching, and we have been forced to be content.

Here is a preacher, however, to whom two long books are exclusively devoted. His sermons are reported with great care and completeness. The circumstances out of which the books themselves arose are clear to us. There are references to his life and his influence in four separate Old Testament books; and the New Testament quotes him, calling him, with an air of great respect, "The prophet."

From all this literature, a reasonably adequate account of his life emerges. Jeremiah was born in Anathoth, a country town distant from Jerusalem by an hour and a half of caravan-journeying. He was the son of a priest, upon whose life God placed his call while he was yet a boy. Thereafter he lived through forty years of wonderful prophetic experience. Five kings came and went while this preacher, Jeremiah, sounded out the warnings of God. Josiah, the great, good monarch whose governance promised glory for Israel; Jehoahaz, who lived only three months after he took the throne; Jehoiachim, vile and vicious, whose influence destroyed much of Josiah's building; Jehoiachin, who vanished after a few short weeks of ruling; and Zedekiah, good in his impulses and eager in his determination, but weak and incapable of executing his will,—these monarchs passed in tragic, royal procession across the stage of Israel's life, while Jeremiah preached. Three great foes flung themselves upon his hapless country,—the hordes pouring first out of Egypt, then out of Assyria, and then out of Babylon.

Through all this vast and moving drama, Jeremiah's figure may be observed. He knew, as a boy, that to be a true prophet for God meant the solitary isolation which he dreaded. Again and again he sought release from his vows, always to be induced by the spirit of Jehovah back into the shunned separateness. He knew what it was to have his words flung back in his teeth by howling multitudes of scorners, when the events he predicted delayed in their coming, or the purpose he proclaimed from God seemed to be utterly repudiated. And issuing his warning in broken-hearted tones to the last, he was finally forced to share in the bitter exile which he had predicted for his nation, dying among strangers, while the embers of Israel's glory grayed into the sombre ashes of destruction.

Yet with all this wealth of material from which to construct his story—with all this history and literature at our disposal—Jeremiah, the man himself, has almost escaped us. We know the life he lived, we know the words he spoke, but we have no clear conception of the kind of preacher he was. What was the element of preaching power which distinguished him?

He was the preacher who buried his clothes. This single spectacular episode is the clue to his ministry. His preaching was drama itself.

It is for this very reason that his books are so difficult to read. There are passages which seem unintelligible tangles of unrelated sentences. This is because, upon the printed page, the words lack the interpretative quality of varying tones of voice. If we could have watched this preacher, and heard his own spoken syllables, we should have discovered at once that his sentences are often dramatic dialogues and conversations in which he takes each part, shifting from character to character by means of mimicry and changes in voice. In the printed book, all these changes are lost. And until this fact is understood, our conclusions are as unfair to him as they would be to Shakespeare, if *Hamlet* were printed without indications to mark each change of person in the involved conversation.

Here is a passage from the third chapter of the book of Jeremiah. In cold print, it seems like

meaningless wordiness. " A voice was heard upon
the high places, weeping, and supplications of the
children of Israel; for they have perverted their
way, and they have forgotten the Lord their God.
Return, ye backsliding children, and I will heal
your backslidings. Behold, we come unto thee;
for thou art the Lord our God."

But think of it as drama. Imagine the voice of
this actor-preacher moulding each syllable into
meaning. The first sentence is tragic echo from
the desolation of Israel. The second sentence,
" Return, ye backsliding children," is rich with
the reconciling, atoning pity of a loving God. The
third sentence exults with the exuberant joy of
repentant ones, who know the blessedness of return, " Behold, we come."

The seventh chapter of the book brings us to
a verse which involves inexcusable repetition.
" Trust ye not in lying words, saying, The temple
of the Lord, The temple of the Lord, The temple
of the Lord, are these." It seems like an error in
printing, when we find it on the page. But hear
it as it comes from the lips of this preacher. Listen
while he intones the phrase in the nasal monotony
of the formal Temple service, mocking the professional priests who think that by much repetition
much religion is indicated. " The Temple of the

Lord, The Temple of the Lord, The Temple of the Lord " becomes a piercing rebuke and a rich piece of inescapable irony. No one who heard this preacher drone it off in the midst of his sermon, could ever forget his scorn. Whenever his congregation entered the Temple thereafter and heard the insincere performance of formal services, the intonations of his mockery would come back to them and they would feel his rebuke.

But he was not content to use his voice for daring dramatic effects. He staged his sermons and made them memorable in terms of dramatic action. See the crowd gather round him in the market-place as he silently builds a crackling fire under a pot filled with a sea of débris and filth. The flames leap around the kettle, the mass inside begins to rumble and roar, and then to boil and sputter. Without a word, while the mob gapes at him in expectant wonder, he suddenly tips the boiling pot over from the north and lets the seething mixture run in a stream of pain down toward the south, while men flee from its threat and howl at its scalding. Then he shouts, in ecstatic eloquence, " See, thus shall the Lord pour out upon Israel, out of the north, your foes to do His will of vengeance upon you! "

He stands one day between two baskets of figs—

one is filled with good fruit, tempting in its fragrance, beautiful to see; the other contains decaying figs, crawling with maggots, repulsive to sight and smell. As people pass by, Jeremiah sings out in the recognizable accents of the fruit-pedlar, " These are God's faithful people—these good figs in the basket; these are the people who are untrue to Him—this rotting fruit in this basket! "

He moulds clay on a potter's wheel, while his voice challenges the bystander and carries the message, " Thus can the Lord mould Israel to His will." He takes a finished vessel, and smashes it down upon the road, scattering its fragments to the four winds, while he shouts, " Thus can God break Israel, unless we serve Him."

Down the street, one day, comes a crowd of Rechabites wearing the strange garb of their religious vow. Everyone who sees a Rechabite knows that he has taken a vow never to touch wine. Yet Jeremiah accosts these devotees, and flourishes before them a tempting flagon of wine, calling gaily in the accents of revelry, " Drink, drink, here is good wine for you! " Of course, the Rechabites repulse him, and remonstrate with him, but he keeps pleading and urging like a man gone mad. At last they say, in impatient roughness, " But we cannot drink, we are under a vow which we dare not break!" The vast throng which has assembled to watch the antics of the mad preacher, is still as death, waiting to hear what Jeremiah will reply to this brave word. Instead, he turns upon the crowd, and calls out in challenging tones, "These men will not drink because they have taken a vow. Yet you, who have vowed eternal loyalty to Jehovah—see how lightly you have betrayed Him." And the crowd slinks away, every jeer silenced, every heart shamed.

He marched solemnly through the highways of the city, one day, carrying, where all could see, a clean white girdle, of beautiful fabric. For miles he travelled in silence, while those who followed him wondered what he was doing now. At last he dug a hole near a rock, and placed the girdle there, burying it with earth and marking the spot with a pile of stones. He made no explanation. His strange act became the talk of the town.

Then, one day, he was observed walking empty-handed in the direction of his buried garment. When he reached the place, he burrowed down into the earth and found the girdle, soiled now and mildewed, its very fabric rotting into weakness and futility. As he held it up for all to see, he said so that all could hear, "Once it was clean and white and strong, fit for use next my body. Now it is filthy and slimy and decayed. Thus it is with Israel, said the Lord."

For days, he walks about followed by crowds of curious folk who observe that he is wearing, pressed down upon his shoulders, a heavy wooden yoke which bows him down. He refuses to tell anyone why, until his moment has come, and then he says, " This is the yoke of Israel's fate, placed upon her by the wrath of an offended God."

While the crowd gasps at its terrible significance, another prophet assails Jeremiah, " God has promised great things for Israel. Israel need not fear nor lament. The future is bright. This yoke is a lie." And he wrenches from Jeremiah's shoulders the wooden yoke and dashes it down into the road where it lies broken into fragments. Jeremiah makes no reply. He leaves the crowd, while they rejoice in the optimistic words of the cheerful preacher. Perhaps they cheered his conquest of the gloomy Jeremiah.

But watch. Jeremiah is coming back. Upon his shoulders is another yoke. This time it is made of iron. No optimist can shatter this. And as the throng catches a glimpse of this new symbol, Jeremiah says, " *This* yoke is no lie. *This* is a bitter judgment from a disappointed God on a disobedient nation. Israel cannot shatter this yoke! "

This was no new message breaking out of a darkened sky of ignorance like a dawn-sun. This was the same old message. But it was being delivered by a man who dared to give it in a new way. Other prophets had said the same things over and over again. The words had become dulled through much saying. Jeremiah did not look for new sharp words. He looked for a way of sharpening up the old words until they were newly able to cut. He found the way of drama. And the old message began to cut.

While Henry Ward Beecher was engaged in a series of lectures on preaching, one of the theological students asked him, " Mr. Beecher, do you have any trouble with people who sleep while you are preaching? " Beecher replied, " I have an understanding with my sexton. Whenever he observes anyone in the congregation going to sleep, he has strict orders to come up into the pulpit and wake up the preacher! " No one went to sleep while Jeremiah, the dramatist, was preaching. Wake up, preachers!

Knowing that he was brave enough to do the old thing in a startling new way, we need not be surprised to know that he continued to do it, even when it began to hurt. Done in the old way, no one would have taken the trouble to stop it. But done in the new way, the news of it soon reached the king. He was told what power the fantastic preaching was having among his people. Echoes of words that were meant to rebuke him invaded the throne-room. And he issued an imperial edict that this sensational Jeremiah was to preach no more.

Silenced, the actor-preacher retired into a study, and there dictated his message to a scribe-friend named Baruch. The book was seized and carried to the palace. The king read it, seated in the palace-hall near the fireplace. As he conned the words, the sheer drama of their message reached him, and angered by their inescapable implications, he seized his knife and cut the parchment into ribboned fabrics and tossed them into the flames while he snarled his rage.

Then Jeremiah, undismayed, began work on a new version. And it is this second attempt, dictated to Baruch in order to foil an angered king, which has reached us between the Old Testament covers.

Across the centuries this vivid preacher shames us for our cowardice. We are so much afraid to do the new thing or the harsh thing. We seek the easy ways of complaisant tradition. We need a touch of the iron of this Jeremiah—and a dash of his untrammeled daring.

from his poetic mind and his eloquent lips. He it was who wrote a text for the American Revolution when he scorned "peace, where there is no peace!" His voice spoke that impressive sentence about "sour grapes which set the teeth on edge." His imagination devised the picture of the "Good Shepherd," which Jesus was to use with such eternal significance in his story of the ninety-and-nine.

To his visions, and his facile picturesqueness of speech, Ezekiel added a daring use of drama in preaching. Perhaps he learned it from his contemporary, Jeremiah, who was sweeping the heart of Jerusalem with his compelling pantomime. Ezekiel once built, in the dirt of the street, a replica of Jerusalem, its hills of dust, its walls of sticks and stones—and in this replica, he enacted the siege of the city which he was predicting. Of course, people gazed in wonder and drank in every word. Once he gulped down his meals and hurried madly away, to show the people how breathless they would be with haste and fear, when the day of the Lord's wrath should come. And when his wife died, a terrifying silence gripped Ezekiel for days, while his friends wondered whether he would ever speak again, and could gain no light from him. When his first words came, they told the waiting crowd that the nation would be silent in far deeper grief, could they but understand what anguish the Lord was preparing for them.

All these considerations make us wonder why Ezekiel, the dreamer, the poet, the actor-preacher, does not loom up more prominently in the company of prophets which surrounds him. But the problem becomes more difficult when we discover that modern students of prophetic trends who have brushed away the débris of contemporary fame and blame, are quite willing to call him " the greatest single influence in the whole history of Hebrew prophecy." This mystic whose words were banned to Jews until they were thirty,—this preacher whose sermons were admitted to the canon by one favourable vote,—this man bulks larger than Isaiah, than Jeremiah, than Amos, than Micah—in the sum total of the prophetic heritage.

And this was his great contribution: He was the preacher who talked about me. The others talked about nations and peoples, about cities and con- gregations. Ezekiel introduced into prophecy the second person singular pronoun, " you." He took my eyes from Israel's sin and made me see my own. He said, " The soul that sinneth, *it* shall surely die." And I know he meant me.

A brief outline of his experience is enough to

account for his startling conviction. His father's name was Busi, " the despised one," a name which some scholars have identified with Jeremiah, the prophet, conjecturing that the two great prophets were not only contemporaries but father and son. Ezekiel means " God is Strong "—surely a wistful gesture of faith, coming from one who was despised.

The boy was trained as a priest in the Temple. He grew up a strict, uncompromising, careful, devoted ritualist, with an eye for all the beauty of formal worship, and a love for the solemn traditions of the ancient order.

Suddenly he was seized as a captive in the great invasion which Nebuchadnezzar led. Jehoiachin, the king, was made a slave, and hundreds of his best people were led down into an exile community on the banks of the river Chebar, in Chaldea. Here the young priest found himself, separated forever from the Temple he loved, stripped of the lovely ceremonial vestments, and the precious properties of ritualistic worship,—an humble lover of God in the midst of a distressed group of his countrymen. The Temple was hundreds of miles away—there was no place for psalms and preaching—altar sacrifices were impossible.

He had been a priest. He became a prophet.

And the change in his official status brought with it a change in his whole philosophy of life.

Hitherto he had dealt with people in the mass. He had seen human need in terms of Temple worship. Sins were met by united sacrifice. Throngs lifted their united petition in one voice of praise and prayer. Now he was to deal with people as individuals. He could not gather them together for common worship. He could only pray with them and for them one by one. Personal work was all that was left.

If he wanted to be helpful, he could not stand off at a distance on a priestly elevation and chant an inspiring psalm of encouraging music. He could only go like a good shepherd, to the place where the one lost lamb was struggling with the cruel briars in the pitiless cold and dark, and help as best he could that one who had gone astray, carrying him back under his own warm cloak to the waiting fold. If he wanted to hurl invectives against sinners, he could not collect his sinners within four walls, withering them with his pulpit denunciations, and then retreating into his quiet sanctuary before the sinners had a chance to reply. He was forced to deal with sinners one by one, like a watchman on a wall, who runs to a lonely outpost and whispers the breathless news of warning into one ear that listens. He began to realize the personal drama which lies back of every single sin. "Sin" the abstraction, became "sins"—the pitiable failures of his own personal friends.

The whole framework of his theology changed. God was no longer a monarch of a vagrant people, judging impersonally from a high throne. God was a tender shepherd who counted and loved and suffered.and sought and strove over the bleating misery of one lost lamb. Sin was not the damning influence of previous generations upon helpless descendants. Fathers and mothers did not set their children's teeth on edge. Nations were not the guilty entities. Nations were made up of men. Men were guilty. God did not blame Israel as such. There was no Israel, as such, before God. The fate of one man was not made by his city or his nation. His environment did not excuse him. He chose his own way, and he must abide by the consequences of his choice. Sin was personal. Men decided for themselves. "The soul that sinneth, it shall surely die."

It is almost inevitable that such new revelation of truth should go too far in the new direction. Ezekiel, who first began to talk about me, actually talked too much about me. He was tempted to underestimate the effect of environment and in-

heritance upon individual choices. Convinced that
God dealt with people as individuals, he almost
completely forgot that each individual is made
up of a tangle of conditioning circumstances.
Glimpsing for the first time the doctrine of "free
will," he may be excused for failing to mention the
prevalent doctrine of "predestination."

But that the influence of his theory was good,
no one who studies the career of subsequent Hebrew theology can doubt. There is a gracious
inevitability which prescribes a certain counter-
balancing process, trueing up an extreme, in the
long run, by means of its opposite. Ezekiel
frankly contradicted current philosophy. But current philosophy continued to contradict him. And
the interplay of these opposing forces resulted in
a close approximation of the truth. Ezekiel swung
far to the left, but he brought his nation with him
in the direction of the truth. And no corrective
was more sorely needed in his day than the thrilling
insistence of a preacher who talked not about
people in wholesale quantities, but instead per-
sisted in talking about me.

Of course, the first effect of such preaching upon
the exiles who listened to it, was a fury of sudden
resentment. It is much more comfortable on the
whole to be able to excuse one's sins on the basis

of a nation's transgressions. Self-pity is more easy to achieve if I am thinking of myself as the innocent victim of a racial fate. I like to think that I could not be expected to do any better than I have done under the peculiarly difficult conditions which have surrounded me. No one feels more embarrassed than the man who is suddenly stripped bare of the alibis which he has been using to clothe his shame. A plague upon these preachers who make us think of our own share in our own sins!

But soon the brighter side of Ezekiel's revelation began to appear. If they were not caught in the inescapable toils of a web of national destiny, they might, by much striving, carve out a worthy career for themselves, whatever anyone else said or did. If life is an act of God, and I am an automaton pulled by strings which manipulate my jerkings, I can, it is true, blame my awkwardness upon the operator who works the strings. But such philosophy leaves no zest in life.

On the other hand, if my sins are my own, I may for the moment blush because of them. But as I think it over, I realize that my good deeds may be my own as well, and I may take a reasonable pride in them. First convicted, I may afterwards be greatly encouraged. This same preacher who levels his finger at me and solemnly affirms that I am the culprit of my sins, also adds the assurance that

> *" I am the master of my fate,*
> *I am the captain of my soul."*

Israel is an impure nation. All the prophets had taught this sombre fact. " Return unto the Lord," they had unanimously entreated. But they meant Israel, not me. And I could not return without Israel. So I was destined to be impure in the impurity of my nation. I was caught in the web of my people's sin.

But this prophet keeps saying that I may return alone. The transaction of salvation is one that concerns God and myself. I may be true. And thus I may help in the return of Israel.

Through this little band of exiles in a strange land the blessed confidence made its way. Despair was turned into daring. God began to deal with them one by one. The spell of mechanistic fate left them. And the emphasis of Ezekiel was the first ray of light which afterwards became the dawning glory of Jesus Christ our Lord.

It was this pioneering message which prepared people to understand what Jesus meant. Without this prophetic tradition, the startling implications of Christ's parables might have been utterly mean-

ingless to those who listened. But Jesus deliberately built upon Ezekiel's thought foundations.
He copied the prophet's picture when he showed
our sins in terms of one lost lamb, for whose salvation God's heart strove, and in whose redemption
the angels of heaven found cause for rejoicing. He
capitalized on the ancient mood when he spoke
about the one lost coin for which a woman would
carefully search. He lived in the atmosphere of
Ezekiel's truth when he told the greatest of all
his stories, about one lost boy for whom a father
waited, and looked, day after day, until that glad
day when the boy dragged his footsteps wearily
homeward and begged to be forgiven. Surely this
ancient preacher was in truth a forerunner for
Jesus. Surely he had his share in preparing
the Way.

Crowds baffle us today. Sermons seldom move
the one person in the congregation for whom they
were intended. Preachers talk to crowds, think
of crowds. Crowds react as crowds. The hunger-
ing heart is lost in the confusion.

The radio flings a voice over a continent, and a
million people listen in, while pipes are smoked and
stockings are darned. When the wireless benediction has been said, nobody asks, "Did that
preacher mean me?" Instead, they remark on the

static, or blame the nearby regenerative sets, or excuse the B-battery, or exclaim, " Doesn't his voice come through clearly? "

Once again let us realize the message of the negro plantation song:

> " It's me, it's me, it's me, O Lord,
>   Standin' in the need of prayer.
> 'Tain't my mother, 'tain't my father,
>   But it's me, O Lord,
>   Standin' in the need of prayer! "

Or, if you prefer, translate it into the moving rhythm of the Gospel hymn:

> " I wandered in the darkness,
>   Weary and oppressed,
>   Till the Saviour found me,
>   Gave me peace and rest.
>   Now in him I'm finding
>   Pardon full and free,
>   Blessed ' whosoever,'—
>   That means me."

You have not really found him until the blessed " whosoever " really means you. To this Ezekiel and all the Gospels bear witness.

X

THE PREACHER WHO SAID IT WITH
BRICKS—HAGGAI

IT is one of the hardest books to find in all the
Bible. As you leaf over the sacred pages, it
often completely eludes your searching eye.
Genesis boldly begins and no one can miss it; the
Psalms occupy hundreds of pages; Jeremiah's
chapters go by the scores; the Gospels are easily
apparent; Revelation spins its final mysteries over
much white paper. But Haggai's is a tiny book,
hidden away, lost in the midst of those of his more
profuse brethren. When you find this little volume, you discover that it contains only thirty-eight
verses. Two pages suffice for its complete text in
any edition of the Bible.

All this textual obscurity is only an indication
of a decidedly minor prophet. Read his verses,
study his record, examine his environment, and
you will unearth little of challenging interest. He
left no romantic story out of which to erect the
structure of his striving, he announced no new

theological concept which the later philosophies have utilized, he specialized in no particularly forceful or poetic language, he mastered no strange literary devices, he was responsible for no novel preaching technique which could help the students of pulpit skill. After we have found his little book, with much searching, and have noted its undistinguished character, we are quite prepared to lose it again, in the company of the greater revelations which surround it.

Yet something there is in these two chapters which at once attracts the careful student's eye. These thirty-eight verses are not without their appeal. Within this brief compass are found the account of four sermons. Each of these sermons is distinctly marked, each one is accurately dated.

Someone must have been duly impressed with them when they were preached, thus to attempt to keep the record of their utterance clear. For human minds cling to dates only when the dates have connection with truly memorable experiences. If a parishioner remarks to me, " Let me see—was it three or five years ago that you preached that sermon before? "—I feel certain that it was appropriate for me to preach it again, for I know that it did not make much of an impression when I preached it originally. But when someone smiles and says, " Why, I remember that as if it were yesterday. You preached that sermon the Sunday before Aunt Emma went to the hospital for her operation—it must have been five years ago— Sunday, October, 12, 1921! "—then I feel sure that the sermon in question really went to its mark. For it has gathered its own associations out of events in the surrounding life, and it has gripped its way into the mind with hooks of steel.

When a sermon is dated, be assured that it is really remembered. And here are four sermons which with all their limitations from a technical point of view, have undoubtedly succeeded in coming to us across the centuries, all accurately dated. Someone had said about them, " Yes, I can remember as if it were yesterday. Haggai preached that second one on September 24! "

More than that, all four of these sermons are clearly outlined. Of course, these brief sentences constitute only mere skeletons of the prophet's spoken messages. There must have been thirty-eight such verses in each opening paragraph of each of these four prophecies when it was first delivered. Here all four sermons are crowded into the restricted space of thirty-eight verses. What is remarkable is the fact that the process of this compression has not left mere fragments of unrelated, dismembered sentences. These are not irregular purple patches of poetic imagery or red splotches of fierce denunciation. These are outlines, as clear as crystal, as complete as structural steel construction, leading from introduction straight through to logical conclusion.

After all, this is the ultimate tribute to a sermon—thus to be remembered as an orderly unit of thought progression. It is poor pulpit art which leads people to recall in after years only the funny stories one has told, or the pungent epigrams one has struck off for glittering ornaments, or the lace-trimmed garments of florid rhetoric with which one has robed his idea.

That sermon alone is a complete success which makes its impression upon the mind of the hearer so that when it is remembered, it comes back as an organized and directed course of thought, which leads from opening paragraph to peroration through a predetermined journey of intellectual and emotional conviction.

This was the happy destiny of Haggai's preachments. Perhaps he fails in literary quality. Perhaps he disappoints the scholar who approaches him intent upon discovering some theological illumination. Perhaps he shows no tricks of pulpit skill. But, say what you will, he made his sermons vividly and completely memorable. And the question which arises may be put in a bald, pert monosyllable—" How? "

The answer is almost as brief. He said it with bricks. He used the most eloquent and impressive vocabulary in the world. Figures of speech may fade, jokes may grow stale and sombre and jaded, pulpit dramatics take on tawdry tints before our very eyes, even knowledge passeth away and scholarship seems like a vain thing—but the preacher who says it with bricks will never be forgotten.

Haggai's people had been in exile for over fifty years. Babylon had captured them, taunted them, stripped them of their wealth and made slaves of them. Suddenly, out of the black sky of their desolation, came the news that they could now go home to their own native land and begin life anew.

With what exultant joy did they hail the news! The songs of Zion, long silent upon their discouraged lips, leaped forth again with gladder faith than ever before. The prayers to Jehovah, long since abandoned as futile gestures of silly superstition, under an unheeding sky of brass, became the rejoicing gratitude of freed hearts. Old men told wondering children what they might expect when they arrived back home. Young men exulted in the happy chance of new beginnings when they arrived back home. They were all going home again—home again—home again—and the syllables made sweet undertones in the blissful harmony of their anticipations.

Now they are safely home. The miles stretch out between them and the scene of their former slavery. Their limbs are unshackled, their bonds are all broken, they have found the promised land of their dreams. But now they are not so sure that they have bettered themselves by their impetuous acceptance of the privileges and responsibilities of liberty.

Of course, they were slaves in Babylon, and no one likes to be a slave. But at least they were well-fed. When they came in from their labour, they could be sure of their meals, in Babylon. Their masters might own them, but at least they kept them. Slaves do not have to worry about providing clothes and shelter and nourishment for themselves and their families. The owners do that.

Now that they are free and in Judah, they almost dare to wish that they were slaves again. Here every crumb of bread must be forced by main strength out of the unyielding soil. The fields are not fertile pastures, but barrens of rock and stubborn weeds. The hills are not lovely rolling mounds of grass, but difficult slopes where good soil will not adhere when the rains wash down. " Oh, for the flesh-pots of Egypt! "

All around them, the grim Samaritan tribes threaten from prosperous settlements of stable strength. With mobile power at their disposal, these fierce warrior-neighbours soon learned that they could allow the returned exiles to till the fields and cut the weeds, and gather the crops, while they waited for harvest time before they sallied forth and took what they desired. Season after season, the fruits of the faithful farmers' toil were seized by these marauding bands—year after year, such crops as they could save withered under the blasts of sudden storms, or fell before the onslaughts of insect pests, as if the judgment of an offended God rested upon all their efforts.

Meanwhile the Persian armies poured through their valleys on their way to invade hated Egypt, and when these armoured hordes had gone, the land looked as if it had been under a scourge of devouring locusts.

With these facts in mind, it is not hard for us to understand how the days of their past exile became a gallery of happy memories. The promised land of their freedom which they had now reached seemed more and more like a dastardly mockery of their hopes. Surely they needed no more misery to complete their discouragement.

Yet here was a man named Haggai, who arose claiming to be a prophet. He knows about the exile, for he returned from Babylon with the rest when the shackles of their bondage were broken. He knows how our dreams have been blasted, for he sees these parched fields and these paltry crops, these pitiless brigands and these pillaging battalions. And yet as we listen we hear him preaching an absurd, unreasonable, intolerable message. He says, over and over again, with a droning monotony that frays our nerves, " Build the Temple! Build the Temple! Build the Temple! "

The first reply to greet this strange demand was an eminently logical one. These weary people said, " Build the Temple? Why? When we lived in Babylon we had no temple. Yet we seemed to survive all right. We need no temple now. Why should we build one here? What unjustifiable waste to spend our efforts and our meagre goods in these needy times, for the extravagance of an ambitious shrine! "

So soon had the habits of irreligion betrayed them. When their captors first enslaved them,

years ago, these people had gnashed their teeth
and sworn undying remembrance.

> " By the rivers of Babylon
> There we sat down, yea, we wept,
> When we remembered Zion.
> Upon the willows in the midst thereof
> We hanged up our harps.
> For there, they that led us captive required of
>   us a song,
> And they that wasted us, required mirth, saying
> ' Sing us one of the songs of Zion.'
>
> " How can we sing the Lord's songs
> In a strange land?
> If I forget thee, O Jerusalem,
> Let my right hand forget her cunning.
> Let my tongue cleave to the roof of my mouth,
> If I remember thee not,
> If I prefer not Jerusalem
> Above my chief joy."

But the circumstances of slave life in a pagan
city had left deep marks on their souls, and
they cared no longer for the Temple. Against
this sodden indifference to the calls of higher
things, Haggai preached without ceasing, and
soon he had whipped them into awakened
consciousness.

On September 1, he preaches his first recorded
sermon. " Bad times? " he thunders. " You are
too poor to build a temple? I notice that you are

rich enough to build good houses for yourselves.
Have you no thought to build God's house? Perhaps these bad times are for your rebuke. Perhaps
this hunger is God's whip-lash to sting you into
awareness. Perhaps this pain and disappointment
is only His way of speaking to you before it is too
late. Begin now, and build! "

The language is commonplace. The philosophy
is ancient, for it echoes the message of Amos with
its traditional comment on pain as a warning from
a kindly God. The demand Haggai voices is irksome, and the task he outlines is prosaic. But this
sermon is destined to be remembered clearly
through all of time. The reason for its impressive-
ness appears in a simple unobtrusive footnote.
" So the people began to build."

Three weeks after he first proposed his plan,
he had them hard at work building. He con-
nected his eloquence with performance. He
geared his enthusiasm to their task, and made
them work.

Soon discouragement overwhelmed them. There
were rumours of rebellion. So he preached again.
" You say you are discouraged because you can
never make a temple like the old one. You say
that yesterday mocks you with its recollections.
You sigh for the good old times. I tell you, build!

The best days are to come. Continue to build. Hats off to the past, coats off to the future."

And the record says, " They kept on building! "

The days dragged out into weeks. Still their task seemed impossible. The hole they were making seemed so small, the plans laid out before them seemed so large. So Haggai preached again. " Is it going too slowly? I know how discouraging that can be. But you must remember the long years of evil with which we must contend. Evil spreads more quickly than good. One dead body can corrupt a thousand. Disease is more easily caught than health. This unbuilt temple has been for years like a rotting corpse in your midst, corrupting your whole life. Keep on building! "

And the record says, " They kept on building! "

At last, they began to grow restive under the discipline of the great task. This huge enterprise seemed too much like slavery. It was requiring such explicit surrender from each individual worker to carry the huge work on. They wanted to be really free. They could not be free if they had to bow before the orders of their taskmasters, even if the task was the building of the Temple of the Lord. They might as well be back in the bondage of their old slavery.

So Haggai preached again. " You are claiming

that discipline is too hard for you? I tell you the only way to do any great thing is by the willing obedience of individuals to their superiors in a plan of organized effort. Zerubbabel is your leader. God is his God. Your leader receives his orders from God. He passes them on to you. You pass them on to those who labour below you in the scale of this scheme. God is still present. This is His task. Your masters are in turn the slaves of God. Organization alone can beat back such circumstances as confront you. Be big enough to take orders. Prove that you are worthy of your freedom by enslaving yourselves to this great idea. Build, build, keep on building! "

His voice dies away in the silence. But four years later the Temple was built!

He said it with bricks. Every word had a task attached. He underlined his sentences with plaster and rocks and plans. His eloquence surpassed the mighty resonances of the great orator, Isaiah. His drama was more vivid than the daring devices of Jeremiah. For he linked his phrases with work that was waiting to be done. He had not finished preaching until he had turned intellectual assent into actual organized co-operation.

The " ear-gate " into the mind is a broad and welcoming one, and most sermons enter that way

to abide for the moment. The " eye-gate " into
the mind is a narrower one, and the things we see
are remembered longer than the things we hear.
But the real gate into the mind is the " do-gate,"
which connects impression with expression, and
guarantees the complete transaction.

Modern psychology insists, in technical jargon,
that " for successful teaching or preaching, the
sensory-motor arc must be completely traversed."
That is to say, the sense impression must reach the
brain, and find its way out again by means of
the appropriate actual response, before anything
worth-while has happened, and before the experience will be retained in memory. Jesus put it
simply when he said, " Be ye doers of the word
and not hearers only." Haggai, who lived much
too early ever to confront either Jesus or modern
psychology, had wit enough to use the " do-gate,"
and his name is held in perpetual remembrance.
He said it with bricks.

That sermon is a failure—I care not how eloquent its periods, how beautiful its language, how
moving its emotions—which does not stir its hearers to do something about it. It has not traversed
the sensory-motor arc. It cannot be remembered.
It has a specious show of success. It may gain su-
perficial approval. But it is doomed to oblivion.

That sermon is a success—I care not how crude its phrasing, how unschooled its homiletics, how artless its structure—which sends people away saying, " This one thing I must do."

Blessed are the preachers who say it with bricks!

XI

THE PREACHER WHO DISCOVERED THE
DEVIL—ZECHARIAH

HUMANITY is always torn between two desires. Any given generation likes to think that it was the first to discover practically everything it thinks. It poses as the great originator. It scorns the contributions of the past. It boasts of its own vast territories of exploration, and marvels that there is so little left to find out in future centuries.

On the other hand, when it confronts something which unquestionably did not originate within the boundaries of its years, it is tempted to push that idea back into history as far as it can. We find it easy to assume that old ideas are older than they really are. We read them back far beyond their historic place. We naïvely conclude that the things which today is thinking have never been thought before, while the things which yesterday thought were clearly understood from the dawn of time.

This human disposition is clearly indicated in our reaction to the story of the creation in Genesis. When we read the account of the program which involved seven days of scheduled events, we first blandly accept the whole idea. Of course, the writer meant just seven days. No language could be more explicit. He goes out of his way to repeat the absolutely intelligible expressions, " And the evening and the morning were the second day." He seems to be deliberately guarding against any possible misunderstanding. This means, obviously, that an actual measured week is contemplated as the space of creative activity, with a Sabbath at the end to mark the beginning of that long series of Sabbath Days which were to close each week that followed.

But upon the mind of this generation, there suddenly bursts the full light of biological and geological discovery. Strata of rock indicate millions of years between recognizable layers, variations in animal types involve the unimaginable reaches of æons of time. The world suddenly seems very old. Crash goes the neat chronology of Archbishop Usher, with its single generations all carefully erected into a structure of world history from Adam to Jesus. Crash goes the seven day framework of creation. Each of these seven days, we now discover, must have been at least a hundred thousand years long.

Not content with this impasse, clever scholars now undertake to fit in the geologic ages to match the frame-work of Genesis, until we are now able to estimate on the basis of scientific evidence just how long a time the work of each day probably did take. And then we commit our final folly by concluding that when Genesis was written, the author meant by days, the periods which we have discovered to be necessary in order to account for the creative deeds of those days. We have imposed upon an ancient thinker, the responsibility for our thoughts, which his mind would never have recognized. When he said days, he meant days. We may differ with him. But we have no right to poeticize the ideas which he expressed into our ideas and then impute them to him without apology. He has been at pains to tell us exactly what he meant. Let us take his word for it.

We have dealt thus with another ancient idea. We have pushed back into the dim mists of history the idea of the devil. We had no part in originating it. It was here long before we came. So we blithely assume that it has always existed. We think of it as a part of the mental heritage from the beginning, we imagine it as serv-

ing as an article of intellectual furniture in the
Garden of Eden.

One moment of investigation would completely
contradict this. The idea of the devil is utterly
foreign to Genesis. Centuries passed before its
formulation occurred. And its emergence into
literature and life is a clearly marked event in the
history of men's minds. It took place in the midst
of the period of prophecy. It was the achievement
of Zechariah.

The preacher who discovered the devil has not
had half enough credit for his achievement. He
really marked a great step toward the truth.

The name "Zechariah" meant "Jehovah's
Memorial." This boy was born and named in the
days of the dark exile in Chaldea. Little did his
parents and grandparents dream when they named
him that before he was grown up, they would all
be released and allowed to go home. His father
was Berechiah, his grandfather was Iddo. Both of
them were priests, both of them suffered the indig-
nities of the bondage when the Lord's song was
silenced upon the lips of the people, and the harps
hung upon the Babylonian willows. Both of them
returned when the freedom was proclaimed, to act
as priests in the re-established community of
Jerusalem. Iddo became the high priest. Before

he died, his son Berechiah had passed away, so the office was passed on at Iddo's death to his grandson, Zechariah.

He was a contemporary of Haggai. They had all come back to their beloved land after the strain of the exile. But they soon discovered that Palestine looked more attractive to them at a distance than near at hand. They longed for the comforts and irresponsibility of their slavery. They chafed under the restraints and limitations of their poverty-stricken liberty. The background of the scene is sketched in the portrait of Haggai. Zechariah was a comrade of the preacher who said it with bricks. They were both young men, bruised and hurt in the disillusionment when their dreams faced the hard facts of reality.

Zechariah's priestly family had been responsible for a broad and deep training in the classics of religion. His sermons were studded with the quoted fragments of " former prophets." He knew the stories of his nation's vanished greatness, he had been schooled in the examples of yesterday's great preaching. The country of his mind was the country of brave expectations and indomitable trust and prayers that were filled with faith.

But he was forced to dwell in the sordid difficulties of this wild Palestine, where crops refused to prosper, and soil was hard and thin, and water was stagnant and scarce, and the ruins of the great city of their former glory rose like gaunt bones to mock their plans. He saw the poetry and the tragedy which underlay the bricks of Haggai.

He was an inspiring and unsparing realist. He could not lose himself in the misty dreams of the past. He examined the structure of his nation with the prosaic honesty of a skilled carpenter. He did not trust to ordinary rule-of-thumb, or a quick glance of the eye. To the walls of her spiritual dimensions he applied the slow, but exact, measuring line of actual, frank, appraisement, and his heart sank within him as he saw the apprehensive failure of God's people, in the discipline of their devastation.

We might have expected the devil to appear in the days of the wild excesses which preceded the flood, when Noah built the ark and mourned over men's lusts. We might have expected to find him in the indescribable filth of Sodom and Gomorrah, those cities where no man was safe from vicious attack even for a night. Isaiah might have been expected to discover him in the repeated assaults of God's foes upon His helpless, pleading people. Amos might have seen the devil in the glittering festivals of guilty wealth which shocked his eyes in the cities of Israel. Micah might have descried him in the cruel injustices which made the poor the pawns of social selfishness. But through all these shocking experiences, no mind conceived of the devil behind the unrighteousness of the universe as God was behind its good.

What experience did reveal this frightful concept? It rose full-panoplied from the brow of the prophet-priest, Zephaniah. Satan is named in the third chapter of his sermons, the shadow of his personality is elaborated in the fifth chapter, and his baleful presence is implicit in every event throughout the book. Where did Zephaniah find him?

First, in the shocking re-discovery of the personal guilt of sinners. Ezekiel had first dared to assert it in those bold sermons when he talked about me. Ezekiel had reduced it to a memorable formula, " The soul that sinneth, it shall surely die." But Ezekiel stopped with the mere assertion that *punishment* is personal. Zechariah pushed on into the still more tragic realization that *guilt* is personal. And when once he had discovered that, he saw the leering devil behind every sin-defeated face, and traced his furtive malice in every bewildered transgressor.

His discovery appears in the sixth vision, which

focuses our attention upon the winged roll of writing. It is a huge scroll, unrolled before his eyes, and it measures twenty cubits in height and ten cubits in breadth. On it is written in great characters the record of each man's sins. Judah does not stand convicted here as a nation, but individuals are cited in this blatant indictment. Men may read here the record of their own shortcomings, and reading, they may know that their fellow-men also understand, and that God has compiled the condemning account.

As this scroll, with its manifold items of shame, was unrolled before the preacher's eyes, he noted each offense, sin by sin, and urged with eloquent pleading that these sins be punished. He called upon the whole community to help him bring to bear the legal justice of God. He roused his fellow-citizens from their lethargy in sin, and spurred them on to take a personal interest in inflicting the full penalties of the law. He pointed out the sure detection of their every wrong-doing, he magnified the importance of each failure, and as the vision closed, he whipped up the nation into a rage of righteous indignation against the easy carelessness by which they had excused their own sins and lightly passed over their neighbour's transgressions.

But the memory of the blighting vision would not leave his mind when he had pressed its lesson home upon his people. Before his eyes, this intolerable roll of personal individual guilt continued to unroll. The big letters spelled out the dreadful evils of the men he knew. The parchment bore the record of the transgressions of everyone. He had emphasized its importance to his nation. Now he could not avoid its implications upon his own thinking. He was haunted by the catalogue of offenses. The weight of the burden crushed him. And out of his perplexity and oppression, he said, "There must be a spirit of evil. There must be a Satan." The fiendish countenance, the clever keenness of the devil, the embodiment of evil, the soul of sin, became stamped upon his mind. He could account in no other way for the pitiable roll of men's personal transgressions, when they knew better and yet failed.

His idea was reinforced by the sight of God's good purposes being defeated by the indifference of God's people. It is the most discouraging, the most infuriating sight in the universe. In it, the devil lurks. Here Zechariah discovered him.

The boasting sins of gilded vice may be challenged and fought. But the dead weight of nice people who are not conscious of any particular

heinous guilt, but who refuse to bestir themselves
in behalf of the good, this is the ultimate spiritual
disappointment. " The path to hell is paved with
good intentions." The devil's features can be so
easily disguised. He is a fallen angel. Sometimes,
without half trying, he looks like an angel yet.
He quotes Scripture with unctuous eloquence. He
mumbles fair words. He deceives the elect. He
works in the minds of the good.

Ary Scheffer painted an allegorical representa-
tion of the scene when Jesus was tempted of the
devil. Satan is represented as a frightful fiend, his
bestial glee betrayed in his cruel smile, even his
horny hoof and his forked tail showing. A Scotchman looked, once, long and thoughtfully, upon the
painting. Then he remarked, " If the devil only
appeared like that to me, I could give him a
tough time, too. But when I see him, he looks
so different."

The painter was wrong. The Scotchman was
right. And Zechariah was right, too. The place
to find the devil is not in the dens of blatant wickedness. He need waste no time nor effort there.
He is at work where two or three good people are
gathered together with good intentions. There he
smirks and cackles, while he balks them into indifference and defeat.

If Zechariah had never discovered the devil, if no one else had ever mentioned him, I think I should have found him and described him in the life which surrounds me. I see him, not in the vile hatefulness of besotted countries which pay a reeling tribute to the trade in drink, and make no effort to escape. Instead, I see him in the heart of America, planning with skilful guile the defeat of the finest, fairest, frankest impulse toward national self-control which has been recorded in history. Here he directs the vicious, selfish, conscienceless assaults of men who wait for a chance to make their fortunes on their country's shame.

I need not go to jails and seek his presence near these bull-necked, heavy jowled, blear-eyed degenerates of our social order. I can find him more easily on our college campus, where he schemes to take the finest young life of our generation and debauch it with easy vice, to the tune of the rollicking call, " He's tied to his mother's apron-strings! Come on, Bill, try it. It won't kill you! "

I do not search for the devil in the frank outspoken attacks upon religion which rise from the anti-Christian plots of atheistic Russia. These are fair, honest assaults. I can recognize them, prepare for them, repulse them, when they come, if there is really anything in the Christian Church worth defending. But when I see church people, bearing the name of Christian, shamelessly indifferent, brutally callous to the pleas of faith, then I know that the devil is in action.

I think I detect the devil in the besotted wreck who staggers into my study and blurts out the story of his sodden shame. Only the devil could make such a ruin out of what was once a man. But I know I see the devil when this broken man tries to mend his life, when he turns to Jesus, when he weeps his repentance, and swears he will be strong and true. Then something takes that man, clad in new clothes, glad in new power, and tempts him with an odour, lures him with a joke, snares him with a ribald dare, and leaves him in the mire. That is the devil.

From now on I shall look for him, not in the gates of hell, not in the dives and dens, but in the churches, in the homes, in the colleges, where the stakes are high and the winnings are rich, where fair hopes and fond purposes are being blighted by his duplicity and skill.

And when I see him I shall remember that hundreds of years ago, a preacher who had lived through the dregs of misery in the slavery of a heathen country and did not observe him,—a preacher who had tasted the bitter fruits of poverty and need without suspecting him,—a preacher who had seen the gilded sins of pagan lust at their worst and had detected no devil there—found him at last quietly lurking, with an innocent smirk upon his dastardly face, in the hearts of God's people, when a great task challenged them and they were unwilling and afraid.

XII

THE PREACHER WHO FOUGHT FOR
HOMES—MALACHI

WITH Malachi, we stand at the climax of prophecy. Four hundred years of tempestuous living, four hundred years of terrifying international tumult, four hundred years of faithful witnessing to God's truth have passed like a pageant before our eyes. The names of the kings seem like the echoes of dead lives, the stories of their foes seem like forgotten chapters of the long ago, but these prophets have lived and moved and spoken as if their words were meant for us.

Isaiah has roused us from that complaisant lethargy which tempts us to find the easier way and has whipped us into a divine fury for the things of God. Amos has taunted us for our silly supercilious pride and has bidden us listen to all truth, couched in whatever crude vocabulary. Hosea has told us of that boundless sea of pity and redemption which is at the heart of God.

Micah has unveiled before our eyes the simple annals of the poor and has despised the cool aloofness with which we dismiss the pangs of others. Zephaniah has bravely risked his life in stubborn courage while he defended the disdained Book of God's Law.

Nahum has sent a blood-curdling yell of laughter cavorting down the avenues of his solemn, frightened world, while he shouted, " God cannot be beaten! " Habakkuk has looked out with tortured, tear-dimmed eyes, from the high tower whither God had led him, and has given us a steadying word of confidence in the ultimate destinies of puzzling things. Jeremiah has dared to take the old, old message, worn threadbare by the years, and has made it new and vivid by his drama and his skill; Ezekiel has leveled his steady accusing finger at me and has made me quail at the memory of my willingness to blame everybody else for my sins; Haggai has made his name immortal by the unique eloquence of bricks, gearing every sentence in his preaching to the sordid, monotonous, irksome task of actually building the Temple walls; and Zechariah has found the devil lurking in the well-meaning hearts of a sympathetic, futile people. But the last of all these preachers, the capstone of this prophetic tradition, the messenger who is to sum up the emphasis of all these centuries of preaching—him we confront today.

We stand on the threshold of silence. Four hundred years of stillness are to follow these centuries of preaching. This one voice will speak, its echoes will sound for a few years, and then the sacred volume will be closed, with its records all inserted. Thereafter it will not be re-opened until Jesus comes and claims the heritage of all these blessed years.

Alexander the Great is to rise in his might, master the world for the Greeks, sigh for more worlds to conquer, and then die in a drunken brawl like any fool. His generals in Egypt are to set up their dynasty of the Ptolemies, and rule the Jews from their Nile-capital. Judas Maccabæus is to lead a forlorn Judæan hope, and to clear by Herculean hammer-strokes almost every acre of his country from the hated domination of the Syrians. Rome is to despoil the national dream with a furious attack which will end only when Pompey has captured and defiled Jerusalem and has placed the Herods on the petty throne of Palestine. And in the fulness of time, Jesus is to be born in Bethlehem, while a Herod storms with rage at the expectation and tries to stamp out this threatened " kingdom " by killing the children.

But none of this strenuous narrative finds place in the Bible until the birth of Jesus. Over these heroic years, the curtain remains down. The last prophet says his word, then stillness till the angels' song rings out on Judæa's plains. It is the last book of the Old Testament. It brings the preparation to its climax. We pause in tense expectation. This is the great, the final moment of prophecy.

" Malachi " is the name by which this final book is called. It means simply " Messenger." Because it is utterly appropriate as a simple descriptive noun, scholars have supposed that the word was not a name, but only a reference to the bearer of this final news. If this is true, there is no slightest trace of this man's personal life. We do not know his parents' names, no item of the background of his career is preserved for us. Standing there at the peak of prophecy, and at the brink of silence, he is " the messenger." Nothing more, nothing less. Yet his very position bids us attend to his proclamation, and the fervent intensity of this dramatic moment leaves no need for human interest material to gain him notice.

His first words breathe the assurance of God's deep love for His people. But the people reply in tones of scornful incredulity. " God loves us? " they mock, " then why does He bruise us and pain us and dishearten us? This is not love!" The wistful words of God croon through the tones of Malachi. "I love you, and these hurts are the signs of My love. They are My only way to tell you of your sins."

It is the old, old colloquy between parent and child since the world began. The patient striving of a father-heart, which must punish though the spirit mourns—and the pettish remonstrance of a little child, whining at the pain of chastening and seeing in the lashes of suffering only cruelty and indifference. But God is not content to explain His thorns of remembrance and discipline. Through Malachi He names the sins which drive Him to His deeds.

"Your priests are lax," says Jehovah. "They mumble through the ritual. They have no heart for faith. They are hirelings for parts in a pious play."

"Your people are cheats," says Jehovah. "You know that of your treasure, one-tenth is mine. Yet you have robbed me, and concealed your deceits. You are clever thieves in tithes and offerings."

"Your homes are ruined," says Jehovah. "Your men dismiss their wives with thoughtless gestures of disdain. Children are deserted, households are shattered, every part of the nation's life is poisoned by this vile contagion. Foreign women are enthroned in the places of your faithful wives. Remember the bride of thy youth. Remember the promise of thy goodly seed. Remember the beauty of a godly home."

We may read with indifference the opening verses of Malachi when he speaks in wooing tones of the infinite love of God. We may listen without a qualm as he indicts the shameless priests, and the lying people who made of sacred transactions a base mockery. We have heard such talk from the lips of the prophets before. But when he begins to talk of homes, we know that he has found a new evil and proclaimed a new crusade. Anything that strikes against homes is a sin against God, against the holy nation, and against the dear ones who are involved. All evils of the sin-cursed life around him can be traced to the sins of homes. He knows that the chosen people must not allow the ancient dream of a love-filled, sacred home to disappear. He hastens to do his duty. He will fight for homes!

The other prophets had all participated, in one way or another, in preparing for the coming of Jesus. They had begun the ideas, had unveiled the conceptions, had expressed the moods on which he was later to construct his kingdom. They had made the road straight for him. But Malachi was destined to prepare his home for him. Seeing the homes of Judah and Israel tottering upon their foundations, Malachi could not be silenced. He lifted his voice and preached for homes. Four hundred years later, when Jesus was born in Bethlehem, a home was ready for him—a home in which love reigned, and a little boy was patiently taught, and a mother's eyes grew big with wonder, and a father's voiceless prayers were answered, and the holiness of God transfigured the humble carpenter's cottage, while a lad grew into manhood.

The laws of divorce in Malachi's day were pitifully lax. The morals of his day were tragically lame. But this preacher prepared no new statutes, and hammered away not at all at the evils of society. Instead he held before his people the picture of a home at its best. He called to mind the happy homage that surrounds " the bride of thy youth." He made his nation sense anew the glory of children, reared in the nurture and the admonition of the Lord. He created with his eloquence the sobbing, thrilling beauty of the home-life of honest affection. And the luring temptations of loose morality seemed like the sordid, bitter things they really were.

In all the chapters of prophecy, no rebuke has been more certainly aimed at us. We have our lax priests, mouthing their lines with artistic cleverness, but having no sense of the truth which they profess. We have our cheating people. Watch America confront the manifold temptations of the Income Tax blanks, and blandly yield to cheating disloyalty. Watch Christians invade a church, and lightly toss a confident coin into the offering baskets and smirk in self-conscious pride. Meanwhile the tithe seems like an absurd demand, and the church struggles along on the pittances of lying niggardliness. (One year of honest tithing in this church would wipe out every penny of our debt, would pay every bill we incur, and would send us on our way rejoicing into new adventures of conquest for Christ.) We have our insincere priests and our cheating people, and the message of Malachi will not fall on barren soil for them.

But he frightens us with his sure attack when he begins to talk about our homes. One of the most tragic facts of modern life is the gradual disappearance of the American home. One out of every seven of the marriages performed this year is doomed to end in divorce, unless the mad pace is stopped. Young people marry late and divorce early. The map of America is a mad pattern of patch-work divorce laws, with different rules obtaining in every state, and hosts of people laughing at our inconsistencies.

Women in industry have gained a new sense of disdain for the monotonous drudgery of the home. Economic pressure has forced up the age of marriage until a decent living wage for a family can be achieved. Children are unwelcome additions to a budget already strained to the breaking point. Wild oats grow their crop of remorse and result just at the wrong time. Hotel life, swarming with its thousands of wandering men, who drift from town to town on the vagrant errands of commerce, is a bitter travesty on the sacred beauty of the home.

Meanwhile Paris achieves new notoriety as a market for new styles in divorce. Modern Americans of wealth purchase their releases while they enjoy the delights of French luxury, and return with their consciences free. Mr. Dooley says that American divorces will soon go out of style among the rich. " How can the wife of a stevedore hope to compete with a lady who gets all her divorces from Paris? Any woman can tell an American divorce the minute she sees it. It don't fit right! "

We may pass strict and uniform laws that will free our country from the mockery of our present system. We may do our best to change the economic inequalities which make many homes mere slums of penury. But we shall not touch the real problem until we have built up anew in this generation a sacred ideal that looks toward the beauty of a true home.

Anything that hurts the home is a sin. Anything that helps the home is a virtue. All the ills of our life can be traced to the ills of the modern home.

Understand me, I do not say that every sin may be traced directly to the particular home in which it arose. I know too much about human life to venture such a rash assertion. All the whooping-cough in the world cannot be charged to the homes in which it occurs. There is an epidemic quality about sin which no one need overlook. My home may make your home miserable, my failures as a father may some day blight your hopes. But the ruin can all be traced to the failure of a home somewhere.

We may hurl ourselves with terrific fury upon our divorce and marriage laws, insisting upon strict provisions and strict enforcements. We may rebuke these judges who descend from their sacred rostrums, chewing big black cigars between their thick florid lips, to perform a marriage ceremony in so many split-seconds, flat, in sporting eagerness to break the world's record for speed, utterly disregarding the sacredness of the transaction on which they place their defiling paws. We may plead for a changed economic system that will give young homes a chance at simple living and financial independence before the bloom of their love experience has been banished forever. We may try to lift ourselves by our boot-straps out of the morass of loose morals into which our generation has wandered, and make the world see once again the consequences of careless sin when it touches the innocent lives of others.

But we shall not really change the situation until we have succeeded in re-establishing that beautiful halo of glory around the most sacred of all human institutions, the home. If I could only show boys and girls what blessed delight is enshrined within the four walls of a happy home, I should need to pass no more laws, and reveal no more stories of physiological ruin and disgrace.

I sat, recently, in a well-loved room in my house, reading a chapter from a Bible story. Near me a little daughter sat, swinging her legs to and fro as she listened. Over by the waste-paper basket, a tiny son, who could not understand what it was all about, played with envelopes and tried to keep quiet. When the story of Ruth was ended, my daughter kneeled and waited. The little boy hushed his noise and listened. Then Molly piped up, in her awe-filled voice, " Dear God, who loves little children, bless us and help us to be good." Our adult voices joined hers in the blessed syllables of " Our Father, which art in heaven."

When the last " Amen " was said, and we all looked up, the son of my love was waiting in silence. He did not know what we were saying— but some day he *will* know, please God. He had no sense of the God to whom we were speaking, but some day he *will* know. I rose to my feet and hurried to my work. But as I went, my heart was singing. And over me flooded the glorious sense of God's goodness.

Take your freedom, if you will. Take your quiet and your peace—take your solitary independence. Take that financial prosperity which comes when you have only one set of bills to pay and one mouth to feed. But you can never know the joy that is mine in the home of my heart's affection. If only I could show the young generation that surrounds me, this peaceful bliss, this inspiring responsibility, this tender affection which is mine—the lures that break homes would seem like the lying cheats they are, and I should not need to fight for homes.

> "'Mid pleasures and palaces though we may
>   roam,
> Be it ever so humble, there's no place like
>   home;
> A charm from the skies seems to hallow us
>   there,
> Which, seek through the world, is ne'er met
>   with elsewhere.
>   Home, home, sweet, sweet home,
> There's no place like home! there's no place
>   like home."

On this exalted plane of spiritual demand, the epoch of prophecy passes into history. When it emerges again, it has become a subtle, all-pervading influence in the life of a nation. It has been submerged in the turbulent affairs of Apocryphal history. But the coming of Christ calls it once more into the very centre of attention.

As if determined to pick up the lost strands of Malachi where the preacher dropped them in death, Jesus begins at once to speak his message in terms of home life. God is to him a Father. The loveliest parable of his devising is a tale of a wandering boy. And the life that follows life is to him a blessed span of joy and partnership in his Father's house. Thus did the last book of prophecy lead into the first book of fulfilment. Thus did God, who had spoken through His prophets, speak at last through His Son. Thus did faith become sight.

Printed in the United States of America